THERE'S NO HAM IN HAMBURGERS

FACTS AND FOLKLORE ABOUT OUR FAVORITE FOODS

by Kim Zachman

Illustrated by Peter Donnelly

RP|KIDS
PHILADELPHIA

Running Press Kids
Hachette Book Group
1290 Avenue of the Americas, New York, NY 10104
www.runningpress.com/rpkids
@RP_Kids

Printed in China

First Edition: April 2021

Published by Running Press Kids, an imprint of Perseus Books, LLC,
a subsidiary of Hachette Book Group, Inc. The Running Press Kids name
and logo is a trademark of the Hachette Book Group.

The Hachette Speakers Bureau provides a wide range of authors for
speaking events. To find out more, go to www.hachettespeakersbureau.com
or call (866) 376-6591.

The publisher is not responsible for websites (or their content)
that are not owned by the publisher.

Print book cover and interior design by Marissa Raybuck

Library of Congress Control Number: 2020931105

ISBNs: 978-0-7624-9807-9 (paperback),
978-0-7624-9808-6 (e-book)

1010

10 9 8 7 6 5 4 3 2

Table of Contents

AUTHOR'S NOTE 1

Chapter One: There's No Ham in Hamburgers................. 2

Chapter Two: One Potato, Two Potato............................14

Chapter Three: Eatsa Some Pizza 27

Chapter Four: We All Scream for Ice Cream................... 39

Chapter Five: A Hot Dog by Any Other Name 50

Chapter Six: Chickens Don't Have Fingers 62

Chapter Seven: Peanut Butter Better............................. 77

Chapter Eight: Cuckoo for Cookies 89

Chapter Nine: Must . . . Have . . . Chocolate....................101

Chapter Ten: Cereal Wars... 113

SELECTED SOURCES 125

ACKNOWLEDGMENTS...133

INDEX...134

Author's Note

Hamburgers. Why are they called hamburgers when there's no ham in them? I thought I could find the answer to that question with a quick internet search. But, that *not*-quick internet search eventually turned into this book.

As I clicked through websites looking for the origin of hamburgers, I saw stories about Mongolian emperors, German immigrants, and American entrepreneurs. Some of the stories were true; some were partly true; and some were pure legend. It seems that when the facts are few, folklore fills in.

Biting into the history of hamburgers gave me a taste of just how much America has been influenced by other cultures. Hamburgers and hot dogs came from Germany, pizza from Italy, and French fries from Belgium. Just kidding, they came from France (although Belgium would argue with that). America's favorite foods are flavored by wars, religion, science, immigration, and innovation in very important ways. For example, the Kellogg brothers might not have invented breakfast cereals if they hadn't been Seventh-day Adventists.

While researching the facts and folklore throughout this book, I found it surprising that no one seemed to know for sure who was the first to make the hamburger, the hot dog bun, the ice cream cone, or even peanut butter. Although each food has multiple claims for the title of inventor, there are no clear winners. Could it be they're all winners? There is a hypothesis that scientific discoveries and inventions can be made by different people in different places at about the same time. This is known as "multiple independent discovery." Peanut butter gives us a perfect example when two men, living in different states and unknown to each other, filed patents for the hydrogenation of peanut butter only one month a part.

I hope you enjoy learning more about the history of our favorite foods in the following pages. I sure did.

Chapter One

THERE'S NO HAM IN HAMBURGERS

WAY BEFORE MCDONALD'S, WENDY'S, AND BURGER KING, there was Genghis Khan. Besides conquering most of the Asian continent in the thirteenth century, this Mongolian emperor found a way to feed his troops that would eventually become known as America's favorite fast food.

GENGHIS KHAN (1162–1227)

Considered by many as one of the great military geniuses, Genghis Khan is also thought of as one of the most ruthless. He and his fearsome cavalry slaughtered millions of people in Asia during their quest to create one of the largest empires in the history of humankind. At its peak, the Mongolian Empire was almost as big as the continent of Africa. An innovative emperor, Khan developed trade routes, encouraged religious freedom, and created the first international postal system.

Genghis Khan's army, the Golden Horde, traveled by horseback from Mongolia to China on their raiding and ransacking excursions. Plundering and pillaging villages made them hungry. They didn't have time to cook dinner because they had a continent to cross. They needed a fast, filling meal that could be eaten on the ride.

According to legend, Khan came up with a brilliant, although disgusting, solution. His soldiers put raw meat scraps between their horse and saddle. The constant friction from hours of riding tenderized the meat enough for the soldiers to eat it. A warrior could be trotting across the tundra, reach under his saddle, and pull out his dinner. The grounded meat patty came with its own special sauce—horse sweat.

Following in Genghis Khan's hoofprints, his grandson—Kublai Khan—invaded Moscow in 1238. The Russians weren't happy about being attacked, but they thought the saddle patties were a good idea. To add more flavor, or maybe to cover up the horsey smell, the Russians topped their patties with chopped onions.

A few centuries later, in the 1500s, trade ships began crossing the Baltic Sea between Germany and Russia. The visiting German sailors ate the Russians' raw meat patty and loved it. When the sailors got home, they tried to get their wives to make the Russian delicacy. The wives must've thought raw meat was disgusting. Instead of eating it that way, they fried it.

Cooking the patties probably saved a lot of lives. Even though *E. coli*, and other bacteria, hadn't been discovered yet, it lurked in the uncooked meat, waiting to attack some poor person's intestines.

E. COLI

There are hundreds of varieties of the bacteria *Escherichia coli.* Billions of them live in our intestines, where they help our digestion and provide vitamin K.

Most *E. coli* are good for us, but *E. coli* 0157:H7 can kill you. It causes stomach cramps, vomiting, bloody diarrhea, fever, and, in some cases, kidney failure. The most common source of infection is undercooked ground beef. But don't freak out! The Food and Drug Administration (FDA) monitors beef production and has done so ever since the Meat Inspection Act of 1906.

We can thank the German pediatrician Theodor Escherich for discovering this group of bacteria. In 1885, Escherich wanted to find out why so many babies died from diarrhea. Scientists were just learning about bacteria at the time and Escherich suspected bacteria might be the cause of the infants' illnesses.

He took samples from dirty diapers and looked at them under a microscope. All the poop he looked at had bacteria, even the poop from healthy babies. Escherich concluded that not all bacteria were bad for us.

For this important scientific discovery, and for digging through poop to find it, the bacteria were named after him.

The new and improved fried beef patty, topped with sautéed onions, became a local favorite in Germany. At the time, Hamburg was the most important port city in the country. When sailors from other countries came ashore, they rushed to the nearest diner for a "Hamburg steak."

In the 1800s, millions of Germans immigrated to the United States and they brought their Hamburg steak with them.

GERMAN IMMIGRATION

More than forty million Americans have a family tie to Germany, second only to Great Britain. But why did the Germans come to America?

In 1677, William Penn, founder of Pennsylvania, toured Germany and told everyone about the religious freedom in the new American colonies. After his visit, German Protestants, Mennonites, Quakers, and Amish immigrated to America so they could pray in peace.

The 1800s brought another wave of nearly five million Germans to American shores. This time, they were escaping a revolution in their home country.

The Germans have had an enormous influence on the American diet. Besides hamburgers, we can thank them for hot dogs, sauerkraut, potato salad, pretzels, dumplings, rye bread, and lager beer.

Who Decided to Put the Patty on a Bun?

Several people claim the honor of creating the first true hamburger. In no particular order, the top four contestants are:

"HAMBURGER CHARLIE" NAGREEN
of Seymour, Wisconsin

In 1885, fifteen-year-old Charlie Nagreen began selling meatballs at the Outagamie County Fair in Seymour, Wisconsin. Unfortunately, sales were slow. People didn't seem to want to stop sightseeing long enough to eat. Charlie realized he needed to step up his game. He smashed a meatball between two slices of bread and named the new sandwich a "hamburger" after the commonly known Hamburg steak. Fairgoers loved this new fair food because they could eat it while they walked around. For the rest of his life, that young entrepreneur was known as "Hamburger Charlie."

In 2007, the State of Wisconsin declared Seymour the "Original Home of the Hamburger." To celebrate the creation of the hamburger, Seymour hosts an annual festival, which includes the World's Largest Hamburger Parade (www.homeofthehamburger.org).

CHARLES AND FRANK MENCHES
of Unionville, Ohio

The Menches brothers were also selling food at a fair—the Erie County Fair in Hamburg, New York, in 1885. Unlike poor Charlie Nagreen, the brothers' business was hopping! One day, they sold out of their sausages. The Menches couldn't let those hungry fairgoers stay hungry, so they came up with a fried ground beef patty that they plopped on a roll. Since they were in

Hamburg, Frank thought they should call their new fair food a "hamburger." Thank goodness they weren't at a fair in Poughkeepsie, New York, or we'd be eating poughkeepsers now. (The Menches also claimed to have created the first ice cream cone—you can read about that in Chapter 4.)

COPYCAT CITY NAMES

When settlers came from other countries, they often named their new towns in America after their native hometowns. Athens, Rome, and Paris are common city names in the United States. Hamburg is also a popular city name and here's a list of all the states that have one: Alabama, Arkansas, California, Connecticut, Florida, Illinois, Indiana, Iowa, Kansas, Louisiana, Michigan, Minnesota, Missouri, New Jersey, New York, Ohio, Pennsylvania, South Carolina, Tennessee, Virginia, and Wisconsin.

LOUIS LASSEN
of New Haven, Connecticut

In 1895, Louis Lassen sold steak sandwiches to factory workers out of a food cart in New Haven, Connecticut. Lassen didn't like to waste the extra bits of steak, so he ground them up and made them into a patty. Then, he grilled it and served it on bread.

A while later, Lassen opened a restaurant named Louis' Lunch. Still in existence today, the restaurant's website tells of a day in 1900 when a customer rushed in and ordered a quick meal that could be eaten on the run. Louis served the customer one of his ground steak sandwiches, which began the famous (at least in Connecticut) Louis' Lunch hamburgers. The Library of Congress officially recognizes Louis' Lunch as the birthplace of the hamburger sandwich.

FLETCHER DAVIS
of Athens, Texas

Fletcher (Old Dave) Davis also claimed to have invented the hamburger to feed a hurried customer at his restaurant in Athens, Texas, in the late 1880s. Davis and his beef sandwiches were mentioned in a newspaper article about the 1904 St. Louis World's Fair, but Davis claimed that hamburgers weren't new because he'd been selling them for more than twenty years.

✳ ✳ ✳ ✳

Who do *you* think first invented the hamburger? Go to www.nohaminhamburgers.com and vote for your top choice.

The common thread with these invention stories is that customers wanted a portable food and that became more evident at the 1904 St. Louis World's Fair. More than two million people visited the fair and many tasted a hamburger for the first time while there. One of those visitors, a *New-York Tribune* reporter, wrote an article about the fair and mentioned a great new sandwich called a "hamburger."

After all that public exposure, the hamburger was definitely trending, and restaurants wanted to cash in on its popularity. The first hamburger chain, White Castle, opened in 1921 in Wichita, Kansas. For a nickel, you could buy a small burger topped with grilled onions and a pickle.

Something else trended in the 1920s—automobiles. In 1920, only eight million cars roamed the dirt roads of America. By 1930, there were more than 23 million. Americans loved their cars. It was common for families to pile into their automobile for a Sunday drive, just to ride around. J. G. Kirby and Dr. Reuben W. Jackson saw opportunity in the car craze. They opened the first drive-in restaurant in 1921, in Dallas, Texas, called the Texas Pig Stand. Drive-in restaurants soon popped up across the United States, with hamburgers on almost every menu.

THE AMERICAN CAR CRAZE

Americans have been fascinated with cars since the early 1900s, but only the very rich could afford one back then. However, Henry Ford revolutionized the car industry with his innovations in the assembly line. This new way to manufacture cars made them cheaper to produce, which meant they could be sold at a lower price. In 1920, the Ford Model T was priced at $393 ($5,126 in today's dollars) compared to a Lincoln Sedan, which carried a hefty price tag of $4,700 ($61,304 in today's dollars).

With cars becoming more affordable, more Americans could own one. Indirectly, Henry Ford changed the way Americans worked, traveled, and even where they ate.

Fast food got even faster when the drive-ins became drive-thrus. One of the first drive-thru hamburger restaurants was In-N-Out in Baldwin Park, California. Opened in 1948 by Harry and Esther Snyder, it served burgers, fries, and milk shakes from a shack with just enough room for a car to pull up next to the window.

Why bother parking when you can eat and drive at the same time? Sound familiar? Genghis Khan's cavalry wanted to munch on the move, and eight hundred years later, Americans were doing the same thing.

Burger joints soon sprang up in every American town and many are still around today. Burger King and McDonald's were both founded in 1954, with Wendy's following in 1969. The battle for customers became the battle of the burgers. Burger King introduced the Whopper in 1957 with huge success. That forced McDonald's to bring out the Big Mac. Then came double cheeseburgers and bacon cheeseburgers and chili cheeseburgers and veggie burgers—the list goes on and on.

No wonder Americans eat more than fifty million burgers a year—there are endless choices!

OH NO! NUTRITION

Hamburgers have been given a bad rap in the last few years as one of the many fast foods making Americans fat. However, a basic burger with one beef patty, a bun, lettuce, and tomato provides protein, carbohydrates, and a variety of important vitamins and minerals. Beef is a good source of iron, niacin, B_{12}, selenium, and zinc, which are all vital to good health.

Unfortunately, beef is also high in cholesterol, saturated fat, and trans fats, all of which contribute to heart disease. The American Heart Association recommends limiting saturated fats to around 13 grams a day (based on a 2,000-calorie diet). A five-ounce beef patty has 9 grams of saturated fat, more than half of the recommended daily amount.

Some hamburgers are unhealthy because they're ginormous. When you see a hamburger with two beef patties, four strips of bacon, and three slices of cheese, run the other way while you still can!

CHEW ON THIS

* According to *Guinness World Records,* the largest hamburger in the world was made in Pilsting, Germany, on July 9, 2017. It weighed 1,164 kg (2,566 pounds)!
* McDonald's sells 75 hamburgers every second, which equals about 6,480,000 hamburgers a day.
* May 28 is National Burger Day.
* September 18 is National Cheeseburger Day.
* According to the Weber's 25th Annual Grill Watch Survey, ketchup is the number one topping for hamburgers, followed by onions, tomatoes, lettuce, mustard, pickles, mayonnaise, bacon, mushrooms, and BBQ sauce.
* Forty percent of all sandwiches sold are hamburgers.
* In 1950, Atlanta's The Varsity claimed to be the biggest drive-in in the world with parking places for 200 cars. At its peak of popularity, The Varsity employed 150 carhops.

Second Helpings

Hamburg steak recipes showed up in cookbooks in the early 1900s. Some called for frying and some for broiling. Sometimes they were topped with tomato sauce or a brown gravy, and sometimes they were left plain. But what all Hamburg steak recipes had in common was ground beef and onion. Here's a recipe for Hamburg steak as it appeared in *Mrs. Rorer's New Cook Book: A Manual of Housekeeping* by Sarah Tyson Rorer, published in 1902 by Arnold and Company of Philadelphia, Pennsylvania. (Note: Always ask an adult to help you in the kitchen, especially when you are using knives or the oven or stove.)

HAMBURG STEAK

- **2 pounds of lean beef**
- **1 tablespoonful of grated onion**
- **1 rounding teaspoonful of salt**
- **1 saltspoonful of pepper**

Purchase the upper portion of the round or the rump steak; trim off the fat and skin and put the meat twice through the meat chopper, add the pepper and onion, and form at once into small steaks, being careful to have them of even thickness. Place these on the broiler, broil over a slow fire for ten minutes. It takes longer to broil a Hamburg steak one inch thick that it does any ordinary steak of the same thickness. Dish on a heated plate, dust with salt, put a little butter on top of each and send at once to the table; or they may have poured over them tomato sauce, or you may serve them with brown or sweet pepper sauce. Where broiling is out of the question, these may be pan broiled.

Chapter Two

ONE POTATO, TWO POTATO

ONE POTATO, TWO POTATO, THREE POTATO, FOUR, Americans eat more, more, more. Bake 'em, mash 'em, roast 'em in a pan, fry 'em up as fast as you can. Yep, we like potatoes and we like them fried the best. In fact, French fries are the number-one-selling item at fast-food restaurants, and potato chips are America's number one snack.

While it might be our favorite vegetable now, spuds weren't always a star on the veggie stage. When Francisco Pizzaro brought potatoes back from Peru in 1532, people didn't know what to think of the lumpy, bumpy things that grew underground.

THE COLUMBIAN EXCHANGE

In 1492, Christopher Columbus set out to find a shorter route from Europe to Asia. Instead, he discovered the American continent. Throughout the 1500s, Spanish explorers sailed to the

Americas, hoping to find gold and other riches. They not only found gold, they also found new foods.

The term "Columbian Exchange" was coined by historian Alfred W. Crosby in 1972 to describe how plants, animals, and even diseases spread between the Old World of Europe, Asia, and Africa, and the New World of the Americas.

Spanish explorers discovered potatoes, corn, peanuts, tomatoes, chocolate, vanilla, pumpkins, and avocados while in the Americas. In turn, the explorers introduced Old World foods such as bananas, lemons, oranges, wheat, and rice to the native people. They also brought the smallpox virus that killed hundreds of thousands of Native Americans, Incas, and Aztecs.

By the 1600s, potatoes had been introduced to the rest of Europe, but the vegetable didn't win any popularity contests. They were actually banned in Burgundy, France, in 1619 because people believed potatoes caused leprosy. Others thought they were poisonous because their berries look like a deadly nightshade plant. However, potatoes made great farm animal fodder. Pigs loved them, so farmers grew them.

NIGHTSHADES

Although potatoes aren't poisonous, they do belong to the nightshade family of flowering plants that includes the deadly belladonna, henbane, jimson weed, mandrake, and tobacco. Of the more than 2,700 species of nightshade plants, most are harmless. Besides the potato, other edible nightshades are tomatoes, eggplants, and bell peppers.

In 1774, the people of Kolberg, Prussia (which is now Kolobrzeg, Poland), suffered a terrible famine. Frederick the Great of Prussia sent wagons full of potatoes to save the people from starvation. But the Kolbergers refused to eat food that was fit only for pigs, so Frederick's soldiers had to force them to eat the potatoes. Geez! Talk about picky eaters!

In other parts of Europe, hungry peasants weren't sticking their noses up at this cheap, easy-to-grow food. By the end of the 1700s, spuds were part of the everyday diet in Germany, Poland, Russia, and Ireland.

At this time, two-thirds of the Irish people became dependent on potatoes as their main source of nutrition. Ireland's rocky soil made it hard to grow other crops, but potatoes thrived and kept the poor people of Ireland alive. Then, the potato blight struck in 1845, and again in 1848, devastating the Irish population. During the period known as the "Great Hunger," more than one million people died of starvation and disease and another two million left Ireland and immigrated to other countries because there was nothing to eat.

POTATO BLIGHT

Potato blight is caused by the fungus *Phytophthora infestans,* which means "plant destroyer." During a blight, an entire field of potato plants could turn black overnight! The fungus also rotted the potatoes that had already been harvested. When people tried to eat the infested potatoes anyway, they became violently ill and many died.

With so many spud-loving Irish and German immigrants settling in the United States in the 1800s, it's no surprise that potatoes quickly became a staple of the American diet. What *is* surprising is that French fries and potato chips didn't become popular until almost a hundred years later. When immigrants first came to America, they boiled or baked their potatoes (likely because they couldn't afford oil for frying).

One Potato: French Fries

Dropping strips of potato in boiling oil finally happened in the late 1700s by some French culinary genius. No one knows which one. Belgium also claims to be the birthplace of the French fry, but we'll stick with France because the Belgians already have the waffle and French fries sound better than Belgian fries.

Thomas Jefferson enjoyed *pommes frites* (what the French call French fries) when he lived in Paris while serving as the United States ambassador from 1784 to 1789. When he became president, Jefferson requested that "potatoes, fried in the French manner" be served at an official dinner in 1802. This meal was the first recorded evidence of French fries in America.

It might seem that this would have been the beginning of America's obsession with fries, but they were too messy, expensive, and dangerous to make. Frying filled the kitchen with horrible fumes and smoke. Hot grease splattered everywhere, sometimes burning the cook. Kitchen fires were a frequent occurrence back then, and no one needed the added danger of a pot of flammable oil going up in flames!

GOOD FOR FRYING

Potatoes have the perfect blend of starch and water that makes them uniquely suited for frying.

When a slice of potato drops into hot oil, the starch molecules expand until a thin crust is formed. The outside turns a golden brown while the inside continues to cook. The high water content in potatoes keeps them from burning.

Chicken, fish, and other vegetables don't have this perfect balance, so they must be coated with batter before frying.

It wasn't until the 1940s, more than one hundred years after Jefferson's presidential dinner, that Americans finally caught the French fry fever. World War II brought American soldiers home with a hankering for the fries they'd eaten in France and Belgium.

The drive-in restaurant fad hit shortly after in the 1950s, and French fries were the perfect finger food for feasting in the front seat of a Ford. Fast-food restaurants have changed the way Americans eat. In the 1960s, the average American ate around eighty pounds of regular potatoes and four pounds of fries a year. Now, Americans eat about fifty pounds of regular potatoes and thirty pounds of fries a year.

KETCHUP

Ketchup is the most common condiment for fries in the United States, but not in other countries. The Germans like mayonnaise on their *pommes,* whereas the Mexicans top their *papas fritas* with *salsa de tomate.* The British drizzle malt vinegar on their "chips," which shouldn't be confused with potato chips, which they call "crisps." And the French? They like their *pommes frites* plain.

The word *ketchup* comes from an Indonesian word for soy sauce. During the 1500s and 1600s, the English imported spices, relishes, chutneys, and other condiments from Asia. The English tried to copy the interesting relishes using local ingredients and vinegar, and although they kept the name *ketchup,* their sauce was nothing like the original Asian version . . . or our modern ketchup.

In the American colonies, the English "ketchup" evolved even more when it was thickened with tomatoes. In 1878, the Heinz company produced the first bottled ketchup and it was very similar to what we have today.

 # Two Potato: Chips

The first potato chip was made at Moon's Lake House restaurant in Saratoga Springs, New York, in the summer of 1853. Did the restaurant's chef George Crum make it? Or did Katie Wicks, his kitchen help, who also happened to be his sister?

George Crum was a talented yet cranky chef who would not tolerate any criticism of his cooking. One day, a customer sent his meal back because he didn't like the way the potatoes had been fried. He told the waiter that they were too thick and soggy. (Some versions of the story say the customer was Cornelius Vanderbilt, one of the richest men in America at the time, but that hasn't been confirmed.) Crum set out to teach that man a lesson. If he wanted thinner, less soggy potatoes, Crum would make sure he got very thin and totally unsoggy spuds. Crum sliced the potatoes paper thin, dropped them in a vat of boiling oil, and fried them to a crisp. Then, he sprinkled them with too much salt and sent them to the table. Crum expected the diner to be outraged at this plate of burned, brittle, oversalted potatoes. Instead, the man ordered more.

The other version of the story features Katie Wicks, George's sister, who worked with him. One day, she was frying doughnuts in a pot of oil while also peeling potatoes. A thin slice of potato accidently fell into the oil. After Katie fished it out, George Crum tasted it and said, "That's good. How did you make it?"

Even though Katie's story is not nearly as much fun as George's, most food historians believe she actually invented potato chips. The main reason is that George Crum was known to be egotistical. If he had invented the chips, he would've bragged to the whole world about it, but he didn't. However, he didn't seem to mind people believing that he was the inventor.

After the invention of potato chips, which were called "Saratoga chips," it became a regular menu item at Moon's Lake House. Great ideas spread quickly and soon restaurants all over the New England area had Saratoga chips on their menu.

As potato chips became more popular, enterprising people tried to make chips and sell them straight to customers, skipping the restaurants. Chippers, as they were called, popped up everywhere. To make a lot of money, chippers had to make a lot of chips. To do that, they used giant kettles. They would have several cooking at the same time. It was hot, slow, tedious, and dangerous work.

Besides the difficulties in producing mass quantities of chips, chippers also had a problem keeping them fresh long enough to sell to customers. However, two innovations changed how Americans got their chips.

The first was the introduction of the continuous cooker by the J. D. Ferry Company of Pennsylvania in the late 1920s. Instead of cooking the chips in a kettle of oil, the Ferry chip cooker used a long trough of hot oil. Potato slices were dropped into the trough by a conveyor and moved through the oil with paddles. By the time they reached the end of the trough, they were cooked. With the continuous cooker, chippers could keep chips cooking constantly.

The second innovation was airtight bags. Before the 1930s, chips were stored in large barrels in grocery stores. A shopper would ask for a pound of chips and the grocer would scoop them into a paper bag. But the chips went stale quickly and the grocers had to throw away a lot of the batch.

After opening her chip company in Monterey Park, California, in 1926, Laura Scudder came up with a way to seal the paper bags with hot wax. She sold her chips already bagged and sealed. Not only did her chips stay fresher for longer, but the grocers liked the prebagged chips because it was one less task they had to do.

WHY CHIPS GET STALE

Chips get stale because frying cooks away the water molecules that are bound to the starches in potatoes. The lack of water is what makes them crunchy. If you leave your chips exposed to the air, especially humid air, the starch molecules reabsorb water from the air and the chips get soft and soggy.

Scudder made the first improvement in packaging chips, but a couple of years later, in 1934, the Dixie Wax Paper Company came out with cellophane bags that were truly airtight and sealed. Chips could now be shipped all over the country and sit on grocery store shelves for weeks instead of hours. And these new bags could be printed with the company's name and logo.

When you think of a potato chip bag, do you think of yellow? A lot of people do. That's because Lay's Potato Chips was the first brand to be sold in every state. Herman Lay was a salesman for Barrett Potato Chip Company in Atlanta, Georgia. He bought the company in 1938 and started expanding by buying existing chip companies throughout the region. Lay didn't just buy potato chips, though. He also bought corn chips. In 1962, Lays merged with Fritos to become the number-one snack food producer in the country. Chances are good that you have at least one bag of either Lay's, Ruffles, Fritos, or Cheetos in your pantry right now.

POTATO CHIPS AND WWII

In the 1930s and '40s, the potato chip business was booming until it almost shut down completely because of World War II's rationing. The government needed the country's resources to make war items and feed the troops. Sugar, cooking oil, coffee, meat, and dairy products were some of the items that were rationed.

Because frying potato chips required a lot of cooking oil, the government deemed chips a nonessential food item. This was a catastrophe for chippers. In 1941, Harvey Noss, president of the National Potato Chip Institute, went to Washington, DC, to lobby for the chippers. Noss had a list of thirty-two reasons why chips were an essential food, including "Potato chips are an economical energy lunch for children," and "Potato chips are the only palatable way to eat potatoes cold." His plea worked, and chips continued to be made throughout the war.

OH NO! NUTRITION

Potatoes are good for you. They have more potassium than bananas, and they're a good source of vitamins C and B$_6$. They're also high in carbohydrates, which are the primary sources of energy for your brain and muscles. Being high in carbohydrates puts potatoes in the food category with bread, pasta, and rice instead of the vegetable category. Unfortunately, once potatoes are fried, they also have the dreaded saturated fat and too much sodium, which can lead to heart disease.

CHEW ON THIS

* On September 13, 2013, Corker Crisps in the United Kingdom set a record for the largest bag of potato chips to be made. The bag was 18 feet tall and weighed 2,515 pounds and 7 ounces.

* The average American eats 30 pounds of French fries each year and 7 pounds of potato chips.

* More than 100 varieties of potatoes are sold in the United States.

* It takes 10,000 pounds of potatoes to make 2,500 pounds of chips.

* March 14 is National Potato Chip Day.

* July 13 is National French Fry Day.

* Mr. Potato Head was inducted into the Toy Hall of Fame in 2000. Introduced by Hasbro in 1952, Mr. Potato Head was the first toy to have a television commercial.

Second Helpings

For a long time after they were invented, potato chips were called Saratoga chips. Here's a recipe as it appeared in *The Ann Arbor Cookbook* compiled by the Ladies' Aid Society of the Congregational Church and published in Ann Arbor, Michigan, in 1904. Notice the instruction to place on soft brown paper. We would use paper towels today, but the Ladies' Aid Society couldn't have used paper towels because they weren't invented until 1907. Please don't try this without adult help. Hot oil is dangerous!

SARATOGA CHIPS

Pare raw potatoes, slice thin, let soak in cold water 15 minutes and then dry on soft towel, covering them with another so they will not discolor. Let them remain until the water has been absorbed, then have ready a kettle of boiling lard, drop a handful of the potatoes into the lard and fry until light brown, stirring them often. Take up on soft brown paper in a colander, sprinkle with salt and place in the oven to keep warm. Put in more potatoes and continue until sufficient have been fried in the same way.

Chapter Three
EATSA SOME PIZZA

TRY TO PICTURE A PEPPERONI PIZZA AS BIG AS A FOOT-ball field. Now, can you imagine seventy-four *more* football-field pizzas? If it helps to form that picture in your head, you can add mushrooms or black olives or whatever topping you like. Can you see them clearly now? Well, get ready for some shocking news. Americans eat enough pizza to cover seventy-five football fields every . . . single . . . day.

Second only to hamburgers, pizza is Americans' favorite food. We can thank the Italian immigrants for pizza. They also brought us lasagna, spaghetti, and linguine, which we eat a lot of as well, but pizza tops them all.

ITALIAN IMMIGRATION

More than five million Italians immigrated to the United States between 1880 and 1910 to escape extreme poverty in their home country. Many immigrants from other countries would pass through New York on their way to other parts of the United States, but the Italians tended to settle in the New York area, especially in Manhattan, the Bronx, Brooklyn, and nearby New Jersey.

Pizza for the Poor

There's no doubt that the birthplace of pizza is Naples, Italy. However, the people of Naples weren't the first to eat flatbreads. Ancient Greeks, Egyptians, and Romans had already done that. In fact, flatbreads, such as pita and tortillas, can be found in most cultures in some form or another.

Cheap, simple to make, and easy to eat, flatbreads with toppings were the original fast food. No forks or plates were needed for these portable meals. This was especially important to the poor people in Naples because they didn't have forks or plates, or even kitchens. In the 1700s and 1800s, the *lazzaroni*, as the poor were called, lived in tiny, cramped houses too small to hold ovens. These people had to eat out for every meal. Most often, they bought pizza from the *pizzaioli* (pizza chefs) who served it out of tin stoves on the street. The size of their slice depended on how much money they had. (Fun fact: If they didn't have any money, they had eight days to pay, a system known as *pizza a otto*.)

When we think of pizza, most of us think of tomato sauce and cheese, plus whatever other toppings we like. Before the early 1700s, however, the pizzas in Naples were topped with olive oil, herbs, and occasionally a cheese made from horse's milk. Tomato sauce, also known as *marinara*, was commonly only served on pasta. It was just a matter of time before some savvy pizza guy spread it on pizza crust. That perfect pairing happened around 1730.

The word *marinara* means "seafaring" and is thought to come from the sailors' habit of stuffing themselves with pasta and tomato sauce before heading out to sea.

✳ ✳ ✳ ✳

TOMATOES

When Spanish explorers brought tomatoes back from their expedition to the New World in the 1500s, Europeans wouldn't eat them. They thought they were poisonous or that they were evil because the juice looked like blood.

The Italians were so poor, though, they would eat almost anything. They found out how good tomatoes were before the rest of Europe. It also didn't hurt that southern Italy had the perfect climate and soil to grow extra-tasty tomatoes.

Not everyone liked pizza back in the day. After Samuel Morse, the inventor of the Morse code, tried pizza while visiting Naples in 1831, he described it as "a species of most nauseating cake . . . covered over with slices of pomodoro or tomatoes and sprinkled with little fish and black pepper and I know not what other ingredients, it altogether looks like a piece of bread that has been taken reeking out of the sewer." That's probably what the rich Italians thought of pizza, if they even knew about it at all. Some of them had never seen it because they avoided the slums of Naples where it was so popular.

In 1889, pizza's image changed completely when it got a celebrity endorsement from Queen Margherita. When Italy's King Umberto and Queen Margherita toured their kingdom, they stopped in Naples. Tired of the French cuisine they normally ate, the royal couple decided to try the local fare.

They chose Pizzeria Brandi, one of the oldest pizzerias, which opened in 1760, to have their meal. The owner, Raffaele Esposito, made three pizzas for his royal guests. One was topped with lard, *caciocavallo* (cheese made from horse's milk), and basil. The second had olive oil and anchovies. The third was made with red tomatoes, white mozzarella, and green basil.

When the queen was asked to pick her favorite, she picked number three because it had the colors of the Italian flag and it tasted good too. Ever since, that type of pizza has been known as pizza margherita. If you are ever in Naples, check out Pizzeria Brandi, which is still open and even has a plaque to commemorate that occasion.

CHEESE AND PIZZA

Everyone knows that pizza is better with cheese. The most common cheese on pizza is mozzarella, with Parmesan, romano, and provolone also used. Authentic Italian mozzarella—*mozzarella di bufala*—is made from the milk of domesticated water buffalo.

Cheese has been made for more than four thousand years and is believed to have originated in Asia. Travelers from Asia shared the art of cheese making with Europeans during the era of the Roman Empire.

 # Pizza Comes to America

Pizza made its way to America in the late 1800s with the Italian immigrants. Gennaro Lombardi opened the first pizzeria in America in 1905 in an area of New York City now known as Little Italy. Other pizzerias began opening around that time, too, all over New England, especially wherever lots of Italians lived.

Pizza was a convenient lunch for American laborers, but they needed a more substantial midday meal than just crust, sauce, and cheese. Around the 1920s, meats and sausages, such as pepperoni, started topping pizzas, especially in meatpacking towns, such as Chicago.

THE MYSTERY OF PEPPERONI

America's number-one pizza topping is 100 percent American. Even though it has an Italian-sounding name, pepperoni is *not* from Italy. If you tried to order a pepperoni pizza in Italy, you'd get a green pepper pizza!

Sausage experts believe it might have been first made by German Americans because it has characteristics more similar to German sausages than the typical Italian sausages. The earliest mention of pepperoni is in the 1894 Yearbook of Agriculture printed by the US government, but it didn't start appearing on restaurant menus until around 1920.

Who made it first? No one knows for sure.

Even with more toppings, pizza remained mainly a workman's lunch until after World War II, when it finally broke out of the New York City boroughs. Soldiers who had been stationed in Italy had eaten their fill of pizza and wanted more when they came home. They started taking their families to pizzerias. Americans figured out what Italians had always known: pizza is perfect for takeout!

By the early 1950s, pizza night became a regular ritual for a lot of American families, and that's when the big pizza chains began to open across the United States. The first was Shakey's Pizza Parlor & Ye Public House in Sacramento, California, in 1954. Then, Pizza Hut opened in Wichita, Kansas, in 1958, and Little Caesars in Garden City, Michigan, in 1959. A poor man's street food was quickly becoming a mainstay in the American diet.

Right after WWII, TV dinners were flying out of grocery store freezers. Pizza makers wanted to get in on that craze, too, but their attempts at flash freezing pizza didn't initially work. Once thawed, the moisture from the toppings made the crust soggy. Early attempts at selling this mushy pizza didn't go over very well with the public.

Finally, in 1950, Joseph Bucci figured out how to make an edible frozen pizza. His solution was to precook the dough with tomato sauce on it, flash freeze that, then add the cheese and meat and flash freeze again. When baked first, the tomato sauce acted as a sealer for the crust so the moisture from the other toppings didn't seep into the crust. He was awarded a patent in 1954 for "Method of Making Frozen Pizza."

FATHER OF FROZEN FOODS: CLARENCE BIRDSEYE (1886–1956)

Clarence Birdseye invented the flash freezing process that revolutionized the modern food industry. He got the idea from ice fishing with Inuits in Labrador, Canada. It was 40°F below zero out on the frozen lake. When the fish came out of the water, they froze almost instantly. Later, when Clarence thawed the fish to cook, they seemed fresh, unlike the frozen fish he had eaten back in New York.

Back then, foods were frozen at a higher temperature, which took longer for them to completely freeze. Freezing slowly allowed ice crystals to form. When thawed, the ice crystals melted, too, causing the heated food to become soggy and mushy.

When he came back to the States, Birdseye worked on perfecting the flash freezing process from 1922 until 1925. He was awarded a patent for his process in 1927.

One of the coolest things about pizza is its versatility. You can top it with anything you want. You can have thick crust or thin crust, tomato sauce or white sauce, meat or veggies (or both), cheese on top of the sauce or beneath it. The sky's the limit.

Different areas of the country seem to prefer different styles of pizza. Chicago-style pizza, also called pan pizza, first appeared in 1943 at Pizzeria Uno in Chicago. The owners, Ike Sewell and Ric Riccardo, wanted something unique—something that would wow the customer, and that would take a long time to eat so their customers would order more drinks. Their deep-dish pie was served in a metal pan and had a two-inch-thick crust.

Thicker might be better in Chicago, but not in St. Louis, Missouri. Pizza crust there is so thin, you might wonder how it holds the sauce! Besides the superthin crust, St. Louis–style pizza is usually cut into squares instead of wedges and topped with Provel, a local favorite cheese.

In California, toppings are the priority and anything goes. Avocado, sprouts, asparagus, eggplant, barbecued chicken, lobster, mussels, duck, or pretty much anything you can think of, and some that you didn't.

When you think about pan-style and some of the elaborate topping combinations, it seems that pizza has come a long way from its humble beginning as a street food for poor people in Naples.

HAWAIIAN PIZZA

In 1962, Sam Panapoulos introduced the first pizza with ham and pineapple toppings at his Chinese restaurant in Canada. In other words, a Greek owner of a Chinese restaurant in Canada came up with a Hawaiian version of an Italian food. Now, that's an international dish!

OH NO! NUTRITION

With its combination of carbohydrates, protein, and fat, pizza can be a well-rounded, nutritious meal. Mozzarella, like other cheeses, provides calcium, phosphorus, potassium, iron, vitamins A, B_6, D, E, niacin, riboflavin, and thiamine, plus a decent amount of protein. Tomato sauce is high in lycopene, which has been shown to protect against some cancers. The crust provides carbohydrates needed for energy. So far, so good.

Now, let's look at pepperoni. High in saturated fat and sodium, it has two strikes against it. Is there anything good about pepperoni? Sure! It provides protein, zinc, and manganese. However, a better choice is loading up your pizza with peppers, onions, mushrooms, olives, and spinach. Save the fatty meaty toppings for special occasions.

CHEW ON THIS

* Eel is one of the most popular pizza toppings in Japan.
* According to *Guinness World Records*, Joe Carlucci set the record for highest pizza dough toss on April 20, 2006, at the Mall of America in Minneapolis, Minnesota. He tossed a 20-ounce pizza dough 21 feet and 5 inches into the air.
* Pizza dough that has been tossed and stretched is called a "skin."
* In 1984, the Associazione Verace Pizza Napoletana (True Neapolitan Pizza Association) was formed to protect and promote real Neapolitan pizza. The organization offers training courses and certifies pizzerias as traditional makers of Neapolitan pizza. The association also hosts a pizza Olympics each summer in Naples, Italy.
* Black olives are just green olives that have been soaked in a solution to turn them black.

Second Helpings

Whether you like your crust thin like New York–style or superthick like Chicago pizza, the crust is an integral part of the pizza-eating experience. Here's a DIY pizza crust that uses yeast to help the dough rise. Yeast is a single-cell fungus. It eats the sugar and then releases carbon dioxide into the dough, forming lots of tiny bubbles. You can't see the individual bubbles, but you can see the ball of dough grow.

PIZZA DOUGH
Makes two 10- to 12-inch pizzas

PREP TIME: 1½ HOURS

- 1 (0.25-ounce) package active dry yeast, plus warm water as directed on package
- 2 to 2½ cups bread flour, plus more for dusting
- ½ cup water
- 1 teaspoon salt
- 2 tablespoons olive oil, plus more for bowl and pans

TO BAKE

- Your choice of sauce, toppings, and cheese

Follow the instructions on the yeast package. It will say to mix the yeast in a bowl with ¼ cup of warm water. The water should be between 100 and 110°F. Too hot will kill the yeast; not hot enough, they won't activate. Stir and let it sit for 10 minutes. If they've activated, you'll see tiny bubbles on the surface and the liquid will swell.

When the yeast is ready, mix it with the other ingredients. A stand mixer with a dough hook works best. This takes a while to get all the flour blended, up to 10 minutes. Some of the flour might be left in the bowl. Take out the ball of dough and knead it on a floured surface. Try to work a little more of the flour in, but mainly, you're trying to work the dough until it's stretchy and smooth. You need to knead for at least 5 to 10 minutes.

Put this ball of dough into a bowl that has been lightly oiled with olive oil. Cover with a clean cloth and set in a warm place for 45 minutes. Usually the kitchen counter will do unless your house is cool. The ideal indoor temperature is 75 to 80°F. If your house is cool, preheat your oven to 100°F and then let it cool a little and put the bowl in there. The dough should almost double in size.

Now you're ready to make your pizza! Preheat the oven to 425°F and oil two 10- to 12-inch pizza pans.

Split the dough ball into two and stretch, stretch, stretch it to fit the prepared pans. Don't forget to oil the pan lightly with olive oil. It also helps to oil your hands as you work with the dough. This is when you would want to toss the dough into the air, if you wanted to try that.

Add sauce, toppings, and cheese, and bake for 8 to 10 minutes, or until the edges are lightly browned and the cheese is melted.

Chapter Four

WE ALL SCREAM FOR ICE CREAM

I SCREAM, YOU SCREAM, WE ALL SCREAM FOR ICE CREAM. Even George Washington screamed for ice cream. Well, we don't know if he *screamed* for it, but he did eat a lot of it. In the summer of 1790, our first president ran up a bill of $200 for ice cream at a shop in New York City. That would be like you spending $5,000 in one Baskin-Robbins in three months!

THE ICE CREAM SONG

The well-known phrase "I scream, you scream, we all scream for ice cream" comes from a song published in 1927 that was written by Howard Johnson, Billy Moll, and Robert King. They were trying to cash in on the popularity of ice cream with this novelty song about a fictional college campus where the students loved to eat ice cream.

Ironically, at about the same time, a different Howard Johnson was making a name for himself with his premium ice cream in Quincy, Massachusetts. His business, Howard Johnson's (also known as Hojo's), eventually became a national restaurant and hotel chain famous for bright orange roofs and twenty-eight flavors of ice cream.

We can't talk about the history of ice cream without talking about the history of ice. About four thousand years ago, people discovered that ice helped keep foods from spoiling. However, getting ice was a problem. People knew how to build a fire and boil water, but only Mother Nature could freeze it. If they wanted ice in June, they had to hack it out of frozen lakes in January and then figure out a way to keep it from melting in the summer sun.

More than 2,400 years ago, the Persians figured out how to keep ice in the desert! They built ice storage structures, called *yakhchals*, in an area that is now known as Iran. They dug an underground room that was connected by a shaft to a tunnel of water underneath the room. The room was covered by a large dome made of clay and plastered with an insulating mortar composed

of clay, ash, sand, and goat hair. They got ice from the nearby mountains and put it in the storage room. The combination of the water flowing beneath and the circulating air kept the temperatures so cold that the ice didn't melt even in the middle of the summer in the middle of the desert!

Ice not only preserved foods, but people soon found that it made cool desserts. The earliest frozen treats resembled today's slushies or snow cones. From some written records, we know that Alexander the Great (336–323 BC) mixed nectar into his slushies. Legend says that the Roman emperor Nero (AD 37–67) loved his fruity, honey-flavored frozen treats so much that he sent servants up into the mountains to collect snow. Their lives depended on getting it back to the palace before it melted.

It's up for debate whether the Italians or the French added cream to their concoctions first, but in the late 1600s, someone included this new ingredient and morphed the refreshing dessert into the earliest version of ice cream.

The French are generally credited with coming up with the "still pot" method of making ice cream. They poured sugary cream into a pewter pot, then placed the pot in a barrel of salted ice water. The cream would freeze to the sides of the pot and a servant would scrape it off the sides and mix it into the middle of the slush. Scrape, stir, freeze, scrape, stir, freeze—over and over again for four or five hours. Usually only rich people got to enjoy ice cream because it required ice, sugar, and servants, which were three things that poor people didn't have.

WHY IS SALT ADDED TO ICE TO MAKE ICE CREAM?

When salt is added to ice water, energy in the form of heat is required to help the salt molecules dissolve into the frozen water molecules. The heat melts the ice and lowers the freezing point of water below 32°F. This is an example of an endothermic reaction.

When a metal pot full of cream is placed in the middle of a pot of salted ice water, the warmer cream gives up heat to the colder water through conduction, making the cream freeze.

 # The Cool Colonials

The first written account of ice cream in America is from May 1744, when Maryland governor Thomas Bladen hosted a fancy dinner party and served ice cream with strawberries for dessert. His guests were flabbergasted that he had ice cream in May.

Thomas Jefferson developed his fondness for ice cream when he served as the US ambassador to France in 1784. He brought back an elaborate recipe for vanilla ice cream as well as plans for building an icehouse at his Monticello estate.

When Jefferson became president in 1801, he had an icehouse built on the grounds of the President's House. (Fun fact: It wasn't called the White House until President Theodore Roosevelt officially changed the name in 1901.) Jefferson served ice cream at some official presidential dinners, which gave the frozen dessert presidential prestige.

The next president, James Madison, and First Lady Dolley Madison moved into the White House in 1809. Dolley appreciated Jefferson's foresight to build an icehouse because she also liked serving ice cream to her guests. Known for her social graces and stylish gatherings, if Dolley served something at her parties, everyone else wanted to do it too. Although she didn't introduce ice cream to America, she did help popularize it.

Cookbooks from the 1700s and 1800s include ice cream recipes. The most common flavors were strawberry, vanilla, and raspberry, but there are references to coffee, tea, and chocolate ice cream as well. The weirdest flavors? Parmesan cheese and oyster. Eww!

Ice cream got another boost when Nancy B. Johnson invented the hand-crank ice cream freezer in 1846. No more scrape-stir-scrape-stir of the "still pot" method. The crank was attached to a scraper inside the pot, so when a person turned the crank, it continually mixed the creamy slush as it thickened. With this new machine, ice cream could be made in about twenty minutes instead of the nearly five hours the "still pot" method required.

ICE FOR THE MIDDLE CLASS

Families of modest means who were living in cities couldn't build their own icehouses, so they used iceboxes inside their homes instead. About the size of mini-fridges, these iceboxes were made of wood, lined with tin, and insulated with sawdust or cork. A drip pan sat underneath to catch the water as the ice melted.

Iceboxes were standard in homes from the mid-1800s until the 1920s when electric refrigerators became available. People paid ice companies to deliver blocks of ice directly to their homes once or twice a week to keep their iceboxes nice and cool.

Not Just on Sundays

Even though it was easier to make ice cream at home than it had ever been before, people still preferred buying it already made. If you've ever turned the crank on an ice cream freezer, you'd know why. In the mid-1800s, ice cream parlors and soda shops sprang up everywhere to meet the demand of the public.

It finally dawned on people that they didn't have to eat their ice cream plain. According to one story, a fellow named George Hallauer went into an ice cream shop in Two Rivers, Wisconsin, in 1881 and asked for chocolate syrup to be poured on his ice cream. What a concept! After that, people started trying new ways to dress up their scoops. Nuts, cookie crumbles, berries, bananas—there was no stopping the toppings.

It's a bit of a mystery how the ice cream "sundae" got its name. One theory is that it was originally only served on Sundays and therefore called "The Sunday." The spelling changed when ice cream parlors started offering it every day. Another theory is that it was spelled that way so it didn't offend churchgoers. But maybe someone was just a really bad speller and it stuck.

We can thank the 1904 St. Louis World's Fair for the introduction of the ice cream cone. We would thank the inventor, but, as with the hamburger, we don't know which claimer to thank. And, as with the hamburger, the Menches brothers are in the lineup.

THE 1904 ST. LOUIS WORLD'S FAIR

Officially known as the Louisiana Purchase Exposition, the fair ran from April 30, 1904, until December 1, 1904. It had 1,500 buildings spread out over 1,200 acres of land. Nearly twenty million people visited the fair that year, with a top attendance of 400,000 people in one day.

In addition to ice cream cones, the fair helped popularize hamburgers, hot dogs, yellow mustard, cotton candy (called "fairy floss"), peanut butter, puffed rice cereal, and Dr Pepper.

According to the Menches Brothers website, Frank and Charles sold waffles and ice cream at the world's fair. They decided to sell them together. To make the cone, they wrapped a warm waffle around a cone-shaped tool called a "fid." After it cooled, the waffle kept that perfect shape to hold a scoop of ice cream. These ice cream cones proved so popular that the Menches brothers went back to Akron, Ohio, after the fair and began making waffle cones at their factory.

There are also other people who claim they invented the ice cream cone, such as Ernest Hamwi, a Syrian immigrant. He sold *zalibias*—sugar-coated, rolled-up waffles—at the 1904 fair. After a nearby ice cream vendor ran out of bowls, Hamwi saved the day by offering his *zalibias* as an edible substitute.

But wait, there are others! A Turkish immigrant, David Avayou, claims that he invented the edible waffle cone after seeing paper cones used in France. Other World's Fair vendors, Abe Doumar and Nick Kabbaz, claim the ice cream cone was their idea. Doumar sold Holy Land souvenirs and used a rolled-up paper to hold the trinkets. Kabbaz thought a waffle cookie in that cone shape would work for ice cream too.

Maybe it was just a "great minds think alike" moment and all these inventors came up with the idea at the same time. We're just glad someone did. (By the way, they were called "cornucopias" back then.)

Ice cream cones and sundaes got people thinking of other ways to improve the ice cream eating experience. In the 1920s, the Eskimo Pie, Good Humor bar, and Klondike bar were introduced. Klondike bars originally came in six flavors: strawberry, chocolate, vanilla, maple, cherry, and grape. Companies experimented with unique blends of ingredients, trying to tantalize their customers' taste buds. One of the most innovative companies, Baskin-Robbins, has introduced more than one thousand flavors since it opened in 1945.

Even with so many choices, the best-selling flavor has always been plain old vanilla.

PLAIN OLD VANILLA

Vanilla may seem plain, but it's quite extraordinary. Because of the amount of time and labor involved in producing vanilla, it's the second-most-expensive spice behind saffron. The journey of a vanilla bean from a plantation in Madagascar (the leading producer of vanilla) to a pint of ice cream in America takes nearly five years.

Vanilla beans grow on an orchid called *Vanilla planiflora*. It takes four years for a young vanilla plant to mature enough to produce a flower. The flower blooms only once a year for a few hours. When it's blooming, workers must pollinate the flower by hand, so a bean will develop. The bean grows for six months into a long pod. The workers harvest the pods by hand, and then the pods go through an intricate curing process that can take another six months to complete.

OH NO! NUTRITION

Milk is good for you and ice cream is made of milk, so ice cream is good for you, too, right?

Not necessarily. If you look at nutrition labels of an average brand of vanilla ice cream and a carton of milk, you would find some interesting differences. Ice cream has more of the bad things, such as fat, sugar, and cholesterol, than milk does. And it also has less of the good things, such as protein, calcium, and vitamins A, C, and D.

To make things even worse, the nutrition label on the ice cream carton says a recommended serving size is $\frac{1}{2}$ cup, which is about the same as a half of a tennis ball. Are ice cream producers nuts? No one eats only $\frac{1}{2}$ cup of ice cream. Most people eat one or two scoops at a time.

Ice cream is not as good for you as milk, but it's not completely bad either. It does provide some protein and calcium, and it's low in sodium.

CHEW ON THIS!

* The first ice cream parlor, Café Procope, was opened in Paris in 1670 by Francesco Procopo dei Coltelli.
* According to *Guinness World Records*, Dimitri Panciera set the record for the most ice cream scoops balanced on a cone on November 17, 2018, in Rome, Italy. He balanced 125 scoops!
* July is National Ice Cream Month.
* July 19 is National Ice Cream Day.
* July 23 is National Vanilla Ice Cream Day.
* September 22 is National Ice Cream Cone Day.
* The scientific name of brain freeze is *sphenopalatine ganglioneuralgia*. This happens when an extremely cold item hits the roof of your mouth, causing a major blood vessel to constrict, which puts sudden pressure in the skull, giving you a wicked (though short) headache.

Second Helpings

You can see for yourself how putting salt on ice causes a drop in the temperature by doing this science experiment.

"ENDOTHERMIC REACTION IN ACTION" ICE CREAM

YOU'LL NEED:

- ½ cup milk
- ½ cup heavy whipping cream
- ¼ cup sugar
- ½ teaspoon vanilla extract
- ¾ cup table salt

- 2 cups ice
- 1 quart-size zippered plastic bag
- 1 gallon-size zippered plastic bag
- Kitchen thermometer

1. Mix the sugar, milk, cream, and vanilla together.
2. Put the mixture into the quart-size bag and seal shut.
3. Put the ice into the gallon-size bag.
4. Measure the temperature of the ice and record it.
5. Add the salt to the ice.
6. Place the quart-size bag of milk mixture into the gallon-size bag of ice and salt.
7. Gently shift the larger bag from side to side to slosh the ice water around the smaller bag. Hold from the top because it will be too cold to hold with your bare hands. Keep rocking the bag back and forth. It will take about 10 minutes for the milk mixture to solidify.
8. Measure the temperature of the ice water and record it.
9. Remove the smaller bag from the larger bag.

Now, get a bowl and spoon and eat your experiment!

Chapter Five

A HOT DOG BY ANY OTHER NAME

JUST LIKE OUR HAMBURGERS, WE GOT OUR HOT DOGS from German immigrants. But unlike the hamburgers that came to Germany via the Mongolian Empire, the Germans got sausages from the Roman Empire.

As the Roman army marched across Europe in the first century AD, they carried strings of smoked sausages as part of their provisions. Packed with protein, preserved, and portable, sausages were perfect for the soldiers' picnics. When the Europeans caught on to how ingenious this meat preservation method was, they grabbed their grinders and started making their own.

One aspect of sausage that was so appealing to the Europeans was how they were made with the leftover pieces of meat that would've normally been thrown away. In a few centuries, sausage making was so ingrained in European culture that people wouldn't dream of butchering a cow or pig without making sausages from the meat scraps.

THE ROMAN EMPIRE

The Roman Empire lasted approximately one thousand years, from 509 BC until AD 476. At its peak, the empire covered most of Western Europe, the coastal area of North Africa, and parts of the Middle East. Besides sausages, the Romans also invented concrete, the Julian calendar, aqueducts, and sewer systems.

The Germans became exceptionally good at sausage making—and eating. It's estimated that there are one thousand different kinds of German sausages: the *Frankfurter, Weinerwurst, Bratwurst, Knackwurst,* and *Berliner* are a few of them. Most sausages are named after the town where they originated plus *wurst*—the German word for "sausage" (pronounced "verst")—at the end. When the Germans immigrated to America, they brought their sausages and their sausage-making skills with them.

MEAT PRESERVATION

Before refrigeration and freezers, humans needed a way to keep meat from spoiling. They discovered two methods: salting and smoking. Packing salt around meat draws out the moisture, making it too dry for bacteria growth. Smoking is done by hanging the meat in a smokehouse with a low-burning fire. Long exposure to wood smoke creates an acidic coating that keeps bacteria from spreading in the meat as well as adding flavor.

To the non–German Americans, the best of the wurst were the mild-flavored frankfurters and wieners. Because leftover bits of beef and pork were being used to make these sausages, they were cheap. In the late 1800s, these inexpensive, portable sausages became the new street food in many cities. They also began to be sold at baseball parks and county fairs. Around the turn of the century, wieners were put on a bun and rebranded as hot dogs. The details of how and when this occurred, however, are a bit vague.

Who Put the Wiener on a Bun?

Anton Feuchtwanger, a German immigrant, was selling sausages at the 1904 St. Louis World's Fair. He served his sausages so hot that they burned the customers' hands, so he thoughtfully provided gloves. He intended for the customers to eat their sausage and then give back the gloves, but they kept walking off with them. The losses on gloves were eating into his profits. He had to come up with a better hand-protector. Anton asked his brother, a baker, to make a long roll that was sliced down the middle. And that is how we got the incredible, edible, hot dog holder, also known as a bun.

What a great story! It's a shame it's not completely true. Anton Feuchtwanger *did* sell hot dogs at the St. Louis World's Fair, but he had been selling them from his stand in St. Louis since 1883. And he wasn't the only sausage sandwich salesman around. There are several named on the food vendor list of the 1893 Columbian Exposition in Chicago, eleven years earlier than the St. Louis World's Fair.

So, who invented the hot dog bun? Maybe it was Ignatz Frischman, a German immigrant who arrived in New York around 1850. He opened a bakery in Coney Island, and according to his 1904 obituary, he was the first to make a "certain oblong roll that the frankfurter men needed for their business."

So, we know that hot dogs on buns were not new at the 1904 St. Louis World's Fair. But something else *was* new at that exposition: yellow mustard. It was common to pair mustard with sausages, but not this fancy, bright yellow mustard. Americans loved the milder flavor of French's new "Cream Salad Mustard," especially for their sausage sandwiches. In 1912, French's had to build another plant in Rochester, New York, to keep up with the public's demand for their new mustard.

MUSTARD

Not only was mustard the first condiment for hot dogs, but it might have been the first condiment ever used by humans. There's evidence of mustard being used as a seasoning dating back four thousand years.

Mustard seeds come in white, brown, and black. Yellow mustard is made with the milder white seeds. Mustard plants are hardy and grow easily in many climates. Before they produce seed pods, they're covered with bright yellow flowers. Canada is the top mustard producer in the world.

Who Came Up with the Name "Hot Dog"?

Buns had been in use since at least the early 1880s, but as with the bun, food historians can't pin down exactly when the name *hot dog* came into being. When food historians research old newspaper articles, restaurant menus, and cookbooks from the late 1800s, they see various names being used for hot dogs, including *sausage sandwiches*, *frankfurters*, and *wieners*.

There's a reference to "Hot Dog" in an 1892 article in the *Daily Press* in Paterson, New Jersey. The article profiled a street vendor named Thomas Francis Xavier Morris, who went by the nickname "Hot Dog" Morris. The term also appeared in a humor magazine published at Yale College in 1895, referring to a sausage on a bun.

The most likely source for the word *hot dog* is from the obvious resemblance between the dachshund, a German breed of dog, and the sausage. When Germans immigrated to America, they brought some of their dogs with them, too, including the wiener-looking dachshund.

THE DACHSHUND

Known for their spunky personalities and supershort legs, dachshunds were first bred in Germany more than three hundred years ago to hunt badgers. Because badgers lived in underground burrows, hunters needed a dog small enough and tough enough to go after them. *Dachshund* actually means "badger hound."

Recognized by the American Kennel Club in 1885, dachshunds are the twelfth-most-popular breed in America. Other popular dog breeds from Germany include the German shepherd, schnauzer, Great Dane, Weimaraner, and poodle.

There's a fun and often-told tale about how the hot dog got its name, and it's appropriately set in a baseball park.

In April 1901, New York was having an unusually cold spring, but that didn't keep baseball fans from turning out for a game. However, the chilly weather *did* keep them from buying the ice cream and cold sodas from Harry Stevens's concession stands. The freezing fans wanted food that would warm them up, so Stevens had to come up with something quick.

He told one of his workers to go around to the butcher shops and buy up all the German sausages. When the worker asked which ones, Stevens said to buy the ones that looked like dachshunds. He sent another worker to nearby bakeries to buy rolls. In a small kitchen under the stands, Stevens boiled sausages, put them on a bun, and slapped some mustard on them. Then, he told his vendors to move through the stands, yelling: "Red hot! Get your dachshund sausages while they're red hot!" They sold out in one inning, with fans begging for more.

The sportswriter and cartoonist Thomas A. Dorgan was at that particular game. He saw the crowd going crazy for the wieners, so the next day, he drew a cartoon of a barking dachshund dog in a bun, but he didn't know how to spell *dachshund*. Instead, he captioned it a "hot dog."

It's possible that this tall tale was spread by Dorgan. Besides being a cartoonist and sportswriter, he was known as the "King of Slang." Some of his doozies include "dumbbell" (stupid person) and "for crying out loud" (exclamation of surprise). These phrases may sound lame now, but in the 1900s, they were the cat's meow.

 ## Are Hot Dogs Made of Dogs?

Naming a sausage after a dog started the inevitable jokes about them being made of dogs. But the jokes couldn't be brushed aside as ridiculous because no one really knew what kind of meat was going into hot dogs. Honest butchers used the good meat left on the bone of a cow, pig, or sheep, then ground that up and mixed in some fillers, such as bread and spices, when they made their sausages. Dishonest butchers might throw in the brains, liver, kidneys, or heart. And maybe even meat from stray dogs—at least that was the conspiracy theory being spread around at the turn of the century.

Back then, grocery stores bought unlabeled sausages from a variety of local butchers. When shoppers looked in the meat case, all they saw were sausages. They would have no idea which butcher had made them, or what was in them.

Oscar Mayer, a German immigrant, was an honest butcher. He opened his shop in Chicago in 1883. His reputation for quality soon earned him a loyal following of customers.

Mayer also sold his sausages to grocery stores. He believed that shoppers would choose his high-quality sausages first if they only knew which ones to pick. He started putting a yellow paper ring around them and advertised, "Look for the brand with the yellow band." It worked. Soon, everyone wanted an Oscar Mayer wiener.

HOW HOT DOGS ARE MADE

Meat trimmings from beef, pork, chicken, or turkey are placed in a high-speed chopper along with spices, ice chips, and curing ingredients. (The ice chips keep the chopping blades from overheating.)

This chopping and mixing produces a meat batter that is pumped into cellulose casings on an automatic stuffing machine. The filled casings are linked into long strands and moved on a conveyor belt to the smokehouse to be cooked. When they're fully cooked, they get a cold shower.

An automatic casing remover takes off the skins and then the hot dogs are vacuum-packed and boxed up for shipping. The whole process, from meat grinder to delivery truck, takes a few hours.

Fit for a King, but Not for a Queen

Because hot dogs were sometimes considered a mystery meat, they were thought of as a low-class food. That's why First Lady Eleanor Roosevelt got into hot water for serving hot dogs to King George VI and Queen Elizabeth of England when they came to the United States in June 1939.

The king and queen's visit to President Franklin D. Roosevelt and his wife was the first time British monarchs had *ever* come to the United States. (Maybe it took them a while to get over losing the Revolutionary War.)

The president and the First Lady took their royal guests to the Roosevelts' weekend place in Hyde Park, New York. Eleanor served a typical American picnic of smoked turkey, baked ham, baked beans, strawberry shortcake, and . . . hot dogs.

When the hot dogs came out on a tray, Queen Elizabeth asked, "How do you eat this?"

President Roosevelt said, "Very simple. Push it into your mouth and keep pushing till it is all gone."

King George picked one up, ate it, and asked for another. Always minding her royal manners, Queen Elizabeth cut hers into small bites with a knife and fork.

It upset some Americans that the First Lady served street food to the royal couple. But the Roosevelts wanted them to experience things that were uniquely American. Hot dogs represented how people from all over the world, with their different foods and cultures, had come to America and melded into a new country, with new foods (hot dogs), new sports (baseball), and new traditions (afternoon picnics).

Even with King George's approval, the hot dog's status didn't improve because no one really knew what was in them. Finally, in 1969, the government stepped in with standards for making these sausages. Hot dogs could be no more than 30 percent fat and strict labeling rules required all ingredients to be listed by name. Before the new standards, some hot dogs were 50 percent fat! Fillers, such as dry milk, cereal, or soy, couldn't be more than 3.5 percent of the total wiener.

Thank you, United States Department of Agriculture. Now, we know for sure that our hot dogs are *not* made of brains, liver, kidneys, or hearts. Or dogs!

Hot dogs are a fairly good source of protein. They are, after all, made of meat. But they are also high in fat and salt, which makes them a less desirable choice than a leaner protein. Hot dogs also contain sodium nitrates and nitrites that are suspected to increase the risk of colon cancer. Sodium nitrate and nitrite are important food preservatives that are used in hot dogs, bacon, ham, and deli meats to preserve color and prevent spoilage.

CHEW ON THIS

* July is National Hot Dog Month and July 23 is National Hot Dog Day.

* August 1 is National Mustard Day.

* Between Memorial Day and Labor Day—considered peak hot dog season—Americans will eat 818 hot dogs every second for a total of seven billion wieners.

* Mickey Mouse's first spoken words were, "Hot dogs! Hot dogs!" He was a hot dog cart vendor in the 1929 short film *The Karnival Kid.*

* In 1916, Nathan Handwerker opened his hot dog stand in Coney Island, New York. He named it Nathan's Famous, and it didn't take very long for that to come true. Today, that tiny hot dog stand covers a city block and his hot dogs are in grocery stores all over the country. Nathan's is also famous for hosting an annual hot dog-eating contest since 1972.

Second Helpings

HOW TO MAKE MUSTARD: Making mustard is as simple as grinding mustard seeds and adding a liquid. The zingy mustard taste comes from a chemical that is released during the grinding of the seeds. Cold water causes more of the zingy chemical to be released than hot water does. The amount of zing fades away unless acid and salt are added. Common acids used in making mustard are vinegar, wine, and beer. Mustard is a natural bacteria fighter, and when vinegar and salt are added, there's no way bacteria can grow in it, which means mustard won't spoil, even when not kept in the refrigerator.

Here's a simple recipe for a yellow mustard:

YELLOW MUSTARD

- ½ cup white mustard seeds
- ½ cup cold water
- 4 tablespoons cider vinegar
- 2 teaspoons kosher salt
- 1½ teaspoons light brown sugar
- ½ teaspoon ground turmeric

1. Soak the mustard seeds in the cold water for 4 to 6 hours.
2. Grind the softened mustard seeds in a food processor, blender, or with a mortar and pestle. It will turn into a thick paste.
3. Mix in the vinegar, salt, sugar, and turmeric.
4. Put the mixture into a clean glass jar or bowl that can be sealed with a lid or plastic wrap and let it sit for a day. It will mellow after it rests for a while. Taste it before sealing and see how strong it is, and then taste it the next day and compare. Refrigeration will stop the mellowing stage.

If you like honey mustard, add honey. If you like spicy mustard, add horseradish.

Chapter Six

CHICKENS DON'T HAVE FINGERS

CHICKENS HAVE WINGS, LEGS, FEET, AND TOES, BUT NOT a single finger. Why, then, did someone decide to name those skinny chicken strips after a human body part? Maybe it's because they are shaped like ladyfinger cakes? Or maybe it's because we typically eat them with our fingers? Whatever the case may be, Americans eat nearly one and a half billion servings of chicken fingers a year, and another two billion servings of chicken nuggets. Obviously, Americans like bits of fried chicken, no matter what they're called.

You might think that chicken fingers/nuggets/tenders/strips have been around forever, but boneless fried chicken has only been commercially available for about forty years. Considering that humans domesticated chickens more than ten thousand years ago, forty years is a blink of the eye. Why did it take us so long to create one of our favorite foods? The story starts with the chicken. Or does it start with the egg?

Gallus gallus

According to DNA evidence, modern chickens descended from the red jungle fowl *Gallus gallus*, found in Southeast Asia. This jungle fowl scratched around the forest floor pecking at bugs and seeds. At night, it managed to fly high enough to roost in the trees to get away from predators. *Gallus gallus* didn't migrate or roam or explore. Being a lousy flyer and a homebody made it an easy target for humans to catch. More feathers and feet than meat, those ancient chickens weren't worth the time to pluck and cook. What people really wanted were their eggs.

Hens lay an egg every day or so until they have produced enough to start brooding. The hen sits on the eggs to keep them warm until they hatch. While she's brooding, she doesn't lay any more eggs. People figured out that if they stole a hen's eggs each day, she would keep laying them and they could keep eating them.

A small, portable egg-layer made a good addition to expeditions. When people set off to explore new worlds, they took chickens with them. On its own, the *Gallus gallus* probably would've never ventured outside of its native Asian region, but thanks to humans, chickens are now a global species.

Obviously, you can't keep stealing hens' eggs or eventually there would be no new chickens. Around 750 BC, the ancient Egyptians figured out how to hatch the chicks so the hens would keep on laying eggs. They built enormous incubators, large structures with hundreds of tiny compartments connected with tunnels that allowed heated air to circulate throughout

the compartments. Specially trained attendants turned the eggs regularly and kept the fires lit. People have been using some sort of incubators to hatch chicken eggs ever since.

THE FINICKY CHICKEN EGG

Chicken eggs must be kept at 99.5°F to develop and hatch into chicks. The humidity must be between 40 to 50 percent for the first eighteen days and then at 65 percent until they hatch.

Egg shells are porous, so the developing chicks can take in oxygen and exhale carbon dioxide, which means the eggs must be placed in a well-ventilated spot.

Finally, the eggs must be turned three to five times a day, or else the chicks will be deformed.

If you do all of that exactly right, about 75 percent of your eggs will hatch in twenty-one days.

 # Colonial Cluckers
(1600s to 1870s)

In the 1600s, English colonists brought chickens with them to America mainly for their eggs because they preferred to dine on cow, pig, and sheep meat. When they did eat fowl, they picked the plumper wild turkeys, geese, and ducks over the scrawny chickens. While excavating historic colonial sites dating from the late 1600s, archaeologists found three times as many bones of wild birds as those of chickens.

CHICKEN SOUP

Although chickens didn't make it to the colonial dinner table very often, they were sure to be plucked if someone was sick. Some recent research studies have shown that chicken soup helps alleviate certain symptoms of a bad cold. It seems the colonists had the right idea. The belief that chicken soup has healing properties dates back nearly two thousand years. Pliny the Elder, a Roman philosopher in the first century AD, wrote that chicken soup would cure diarrhea. Maimonides, a twelfth-century Jewish physician and teacher, prescribed chicken soup as a cure for leprosy. It's not a cure for leprosy (which is a bacterial infection), but it probably helped the patients feel better.

The opposite was found at excavations around slave cabins on Virginian plantations. There, chicken bones were in the majority. Since the beginning of slavery in America, owners allowed their slaves to raise chickens and grow vegetables. The more food the slaves could produce for themselves, the less the owners had to provide.

"Yard birds," as chickens were sometimes called, roamed the farms, scratching in the dirt and cattle manure for bugs. Hanging around cow poop earned them another nickname—"dung hens," which made them even more unappealing to plantation owners.

The slaves became expert poultry farmers and poultry cooks. Since slave women typically cooked the meals for plantation owners, they made what they knew how to make the best. Their fried chicken, prepared with their

West African techniques, became a favorite dish among many plantation owners. Ironically, the owners had to buy the chicken from someone if they wanted it for dinner, so they bought it from their slaves, who then cooked it for them. Some savvy slaves earned enough from this side business to buy their freedom.

In 1824, Mary Randolph, a white woman, published the first recipe for "Southern Fried Chicken" in her cookbook *The Virginia Housewife*. Randolph had been a prominent society hostess in Richmond, Virginia, until her name became associated with a slave revolt. Her husband lost his job because of the scandal and they opened a boardinghouse to support themselves. Her recipe, which called for the chicken pieces to be coated in flour, sprinkled with salt, and then fried in lard, was obviously influenced by slave cooks. It became the basis for fried chicken in America.

The Lean Years
(1870s to 1920s)

Even though people loved fried chicken, it wasn't served very often because it required so much work to prepare and cook. Recipes from the late 1800s start with detailed instructions about slaughtering the hen, plucking it, taking out the guts and gizzards, and then cutting it into pieces. All of that had to be done before the actual battering and frying. Back then, kids got chicken wings and legs, but no chicken fingers. Separating the meat from the bone added another step to an already laborious process.

Availability of chickens was an issue for city dwellers. Country folk kept chickens on their farm and could grab one whenever they wanted, but city folk had to buy their poultry from a butcher shop. With no refrigeration, and transportation consisting of horses and wagons, getting those yard birds from the farm to an urban table was tricky.

Winter also affected supply. Chickens didn't lay as many eggs during cold weather, which meant there were fewer chicks to grow up to be sold at butcher shops. Because of the lack of steady supply, chicken cost twice the amount of beef or pork. Expensive, hard to find, and difficult to prepare, chicken was only served on special occasions in the cities.

In the early 1900s, Americans ate about 10 pounds of chicken per person per year. Today, Americans eat more than 90 pounds of chicken per person per year. What changed? Believe it or not, the discovery of vitamins.

THE DISCOVERY OF VITAMINS

Scientists had been working for years to understand the causes of diseases such as rickets, scurvy, and beriberi in humans. A breakthrough came in 1911 when Casmir Funk, a Polish scientist, theorized that foods might contain "vital amines" necessary to health. Many scientists in several countries conducted a flurry of experiments testing his theory. They concluded that he was right. Vitamin A was discovered in 1913 and in a few years later, vitamins B, C, and D, in that order. Funk's term *vital amines* became *vitamins*.

Birds, reptiles, amphibians, and most mammals, including humans, need vitamin D. Using a form of photosynthesis, animals make vitamin D when sunlight is absorbed through their skin. In some parts of the United States, though, the sun isn't strong enough during the winter months for the production of vitamin D to occur. In birds and mammals, a symptom of vitamin D deficiency is soft, deformed bones. (In humans, it's called rickets.)

Farmers kept their chickens in the barn during the winter months to protect them from the weather and from predators, but hens didn't do very well inside. They laid fewer eggs, and those chicks that hatched had "leg weakness," what they called rickets in chickens. After the discovery of vitamins, farmers began adding cod liver oil (it's high in vitamins A and D) to the chickens' feed. The hens laid more eggs, and the chicks grew bigger and stronger in a shorter amount of time. With this new miracle feed, farmers could keep their poultry inside all the time and breed them year-round.

In addition to the vitamin supplements, the 1920s and '30s brought a wave of technological advances that helped the chicken industry. Refrigeration, trucks, highways, and electricity all contributed to a much more efficient supply chain. It became very easy to get the chicken from farm to the urban table.

The Broiler Boom
(1940s to 1960s)

Other advances in medicine helped grow the chicken industry—and the chicken itself. Antibiotics and vaccines helped fight the illnesses and frequent infections that were common in poultry. By breeding different kinds of chickens together, farmers were able to produce fowl that were twice as big as their colonial ancestors, which meant twice the edible meat. Chickens raised for meat are called broilers.

When farmers capitalized on these advances, production boomed. In 1934, eight million broilers were raised. In 1953, that number exploded to 486 million. Not only was chicken meat readily available in grocery stores, it was also being sold ready to cook in packages of legs, thighs, wings, or breasts, or a whole bird for roasting, which made it much more attractive to homemakers.

It was easier than ever before to make fried chicken, but it was still a chore and Americans liked to buy it already cooked when they could. One of their favorite places to get it was Kentucky Fried Chicken. This national restaurant chain began with a small café in Corbin, Kentucky, in 1930 and grew into the largest fast-food company in America by 1963. It's now the second-largest chain in the world behind McDonald's.

KENTUCKY FRIED CHICKEN

With his secret recipe of eleven herbs and spices, Harland Sanders sold his fried chicken from a roadside café in Corbin, Kentucky, in the early 1930s. His chicken became so popular that the governor of Kentucky awarded him the honorary title of colonel. Part of his secret recipe was his method of frying chicken in a specially modified pressure cooker. Colonel Sanders was frustrated with the time it took to fry chicken in a pan, and he didn't like deep fryers. After countless trials, he finally came up with the perfect method of frying in a pressure cooker. Not only did it cut the cooking time in half, but the chicken came out crunchy on the outside and juicy on the inside.

The first KFC franchise opened in Salt Lake City, Utah, in 1952. By 1964, there were six hundred KFC restaurants in the United States.

Even with the popularity of fried chicken flying high, and Americans consuming more poultry at home than ever before, farmers were struggling to make a profit because they were producing chickens faster than grocery stores could sell them, which kept prices low. They needed help. Dr. Robert Baker, a Cornell University scientist, came to the rescue.

Having grown up during the Great Depression on his parents' struggling apple farm, Baker knew firsthand how hard it was to make a living by farming. He hoped to develop more uses for chicken to increase demand, so the farmers could get a higher price at market. In 1959, Dr. Baker set up a poultry products laboratory at Cornell University. With a team of scientists and chefs, he developed over fifty chicken products, including franks, meat loaf, hash, bologna, chili, and, the most important of all, the first nugget—the Chicken Crispie.

Creating the Chicken Crispie for mass production required solving a couple of problems. One was getting the meat off the bone in an economical and timely way. The other was getting the batter to stick to chicken throughout the freezing and frying stages. Dr. Baker and his team finally succeeded. Baker published a paper outlining the process in the *Cornell Bulletin* in 1963, hoping a large food corporation would read it and run with it. They didn't. Americans still didn't have access to commercially made boneless chicken fingers or nuggets—but that would change soon enough.

 # The Boneless Boom
(1970s to 1980s)

Chicken consumption saw a bump when red meat got blamed for heart disease. In the 1950s, heart disease had become almost epidemic in America and early studies linked eating red meat to increased risk of heart attack and stroke.

HEART DISEASE

By the 1950s, heart attacks and strokes killed more Americans than all forms of cancer combined. Doctors wanted to know why. Formed in 1924, the American Heart Association (AHA) sponsored research into the causes of heart disease. In 1956, scientists discovered a link between cholesterol and heart disease. In 1961, the AHA released its first dietary guidelines limiting saturated fats—which were prevalent in red meats.

In 1977, the United States government told Americans to quit eating so much beef and to start eating more chicken and fish, which contained leaner proteins and less saturated fats. The head honchos at McDonald's freaked. They had to come up with a chicken product pronto because it looked as though hamburger sales were going to plummet.

Even before the 1977 government announcement, McDonald's knew it needed to expand its menu to include chicken. In 1976, the founder of McDonald's, Ray Kroc, hired Rene Arend, a French-trained chef from Luxembourg, to create a chicken menu item. For a couple of years, Arend experimented with chicken dishes. He tried potpies, but they failed market testing. Then, he made fried chicken, and even though it was delicious, it wasn't good enough to steal Kentucky Fried Chicken's customers.

In early 1979, Fred Turner, the chairman of the McDonald's board, happened to pass Arend in the hallway and said, "Why not a chicken nugget?" By that afternoon, Arend presented Turner samples of bite-size, breaded, and deep-fried chicken nuggets. Turner knew a winner when he tasted it. Now, all they had to do was to figure out how to mass produce it.

Turner assembled a team of industry experts to work out how to make chicken nuggets as quickly as possible. The Chicken McNugget SWAT team (their nickname) faced the same problems with deboning and batter as Dr. Baker had. It's a shame they didn't know about Chicken Crispies, because they might have saved some time.

The SWAT team figured it out in a surprisingly short time, and by 1980, they market-tested the Chicken McNugget at fifteen McDonald's locations in Knoxville, Tennessee. They were an instant success. Other McDonald's locations heard about McNuggets and wanted them too. To meet demand, the company built a new manufacturing plant. As soon as it opened, it ran seven days a week. In less than one year, McDonald's had sold more chicken than any other restaurant in America, except Kentucky Fried Chicken.

That's where we got chicken nuggets, but what about chicken fingers? A couple of restaurants claim to be the first to serve this form of fried fowl.

Spanky's in Savannah, Georgia, proudly boasts that it's the "Home of the Original Chicken Finger." Three friends—Alben Yarbrough, Ansley Williams, and Dusty Yarbrough—opened Spanky's in 1976 as a pizza and beer joint. But Alben insisted that they offer at least one chicken item. While making a chicken breast sandwich, he cut off the edges of the chicken so it would fit on a bun. He took the scraps, breaded and seasoned them, then deep-fried them. He'd discovered the perfect chicken dish to add to their menu. When asked why they called them "chicken fingers," Ansley Williams answered, "We called them Chicken Fingers because it sounded a lot more appetizing than Chicken Toes!"

Another early chicken finger restaurant contender was Guthrie's in Haleyville, Alabama. The original Guthrie's restaurant opened in 1965 with a full menu including burgers, barbecue, and fried chicken. It started serving chicken fingers in 1978. The fingers were so popular, a second restaurant, Guthrie's Golden Fried Chicken Fingers, was opened in Auburn, Alabama, in 1982, selling *only* chicken and fries. It claims to be "America's First Chicken Finger Restaurant."

Both restaurants were ahead of the mad rush to create a boneless fried chicken product after the Chicken McNugget came out in 1980. From small diners to corporate fast-food chains, restaurants quickly created their own versions. After ten thousand years of chickens being a domesticated animal, people finally got unlimited access to the chicken fingers, nuggets, tenders, strips, or whatever else you want to call them.

While chicken was once touted as a healthier option than beef, we now know that fried chicken also has cholesterol and saturated fat. Chicken nuggets, in fact, aren't healthier than a hamburger. However, chicken *is* a good source of protein, vitamins B_3 and B_6, and selenium. As with all fried foods, eat chicken nuggets in moderation, or better yet, go grilled.

CHEW ON THIS

* Did you know that chickens are related to the mighty *Tyrannosaurus rex*? In 2003, scientists extracted molecules of collagen from a T-rex bone and compared it to living creatures, including humans. Chicken and ostriches were the closest match.

* There are more than 50 billion chickens on earth—the largest population of any feathered species.

* Americans eat nearly 6 million pounds of chicken every hour of every day.

* After receiving some Cochin China fowl as a gift, England's Queen Victoria became fascinated with exotic chickens and started collecting them. By 1845, "Hen Fever" spread to the English and American upper classes, culminating in the 1849 Boston Poultry Show attended by over 10,000 spectators.

* There are more than 500 breeds of chicken in the world. The American Poultry Association recognizes 120.

* The Ameraucana chicken lays blue eggs.

* Looking like a puffball, the American silkie has feathers that feel like fur. It's beautiful on the outside, but strange on the inside with dark blue skin and bones. Even the meat has a blue hue.

* In China, the favorite part of the chicken to eat is the feet. The Chinese call them "phoenix talons" and they can be prepared in dozens of ways. Chicken feet are so popular there that they cost more than regular poultry meat.

Second Helpings

Going gluten-free means you must give up a lot of foods, including chicken nuggets. This recipe doesn't try to replicate the standard restaurant fare, but is rather a completely new version and delicious in its own way.

GLUTEN-FREE CHICKEN NUGGETS

- Cooking spray, for pan
- 1 (8-ounce) bag nonridged potato chips
- 1 pound skinless chicken breasts
- ¼ teaspoon salt
- ¼ teaspoon pepper
- ⅛ teaspoon paprika
- 1 tablespoon mayonnaise

Preheat the oven to 375°F. Spray a baking sheet with cooking spray.

Crush the chips into fine crumbs. Cut the chicken into bite-size pieces and put in a bowl. Sprinkle the chicken with the salt, pepper, and paprika. Add the mayonnaise and toss until the chicken pieces are coated. Roll the chicken pieces in the potato chip crumbs until covered. Place in a single layer on the prepared baking sheet. Bake for 30 to 35 minutes, or until lightly browned. Be sure and throw away any unused chip crumbs, as they will be contaminated with raw chicken!

Chapter Seven
PEANUT BUTTER BETTER

IT MAKES BREAD BETTER. IT MAKES COOKIES BETTER. IT even makes celery sticks better. You name it, and peanut butter most likely makes it better. Sure, we like plain peanuts, too, but there's something extra special about that gooey, creamy, sticky stuff that keeps us dipping our spoon in the jar.

It's kind of funny that peanut butter isn't really butter and peanuts are not really nuts. They're actually in the same plant family as peas and beans, called legumes (leh-gyoomz). We should probably call peanut butter "legume paste," but that sounds disgusting.

THE PECULIAR PEANUT PLANT

When a peanut is planted, it sprouts pairs of leaves shaped like a clam shell. The leaves open in the morning and close at night. After one month, small yellow and red flowers bloom.

> They live for one day and then fall off. Where the flower used to be, a shoot, called a peg, develops. The peg turns down and goes underground and eventually grows into a peanut.
>
> There is only one other plant that flowers aboveground but grows the fruit below ground, and that is the bambarra groundnut of West Africa.

People have been growing peanuts for nearly four thousand years. Scientists believe the first ones came from South America. When Spanish explorers discovered the Americas in the 1500s peanuts were one of the exotic new foods they brought back to Europe along with chocolate, vanilla, potatoes, and tomatoes.

As trading routes became established between Europe, Asia, and Africa in the 1600s, peanuts spread like wildfire, especially in Africa and Asia. They grew so well in West Africa, they became a main food source there. When West Africans were captured and shipped to America as slaves, they brought peanuts with them. Rarely given enough to eat, the slaves grew peanuts behind their slave cabins to supplement their diet.

At the beginning of the 1800s, peanuts started on a career track as a snack food. They were popular with street vendors because they were cheap, easy to roast, and could be sold for more than double the cost. They were popular with the customers, too, especially at circuses and fairs. By the 1870s, roasted peanuts were as much a part of the circus experience as the clowns. The myth that elephants love peanuts (they don't) is thought to be tied to promotional materials from 1885 for Jumbo the Elephant of P. T. Barnum's "The Greatest Show on Earth."

As baseball grew into America's favorite sport after the Civil War, peanut sales grew with it. At first, roasted, unshelled peanuts were sold because they made more profit. Unfortunately, baseball fans dumped the empty peanut shells on the ground, making a big mess. Park owners soon realized they were spending more money cleaning up the shells then they were making in sales. That started the shift to shelled peanuts. Whether shelled or unshelled, by the late 1880s, peanuts were firmly established as America's number one snack food.

Peanuts Get Creamed

Who was the first person to make peanut butter, then? According to Dr. John Harvey Kellogg, it was him. Yes, he was one of the Kellogg brothers who invented cornflakes (and you will read more about him and his brother in Chapter 10). Dr. Kellogg ran the Battle Creek Sanitarium in Michigan. Sanitariums were places where people went to feel better and get healthier—sort of a cross between a hospital and a hotel.

To some people, peanuts were only a cheap snack, but to a health nut like Dr. Kellogg, they were a vegetarian's treasure. Dr. Kellogg believed in a plant-based diet and he thought the protein-packed peanut would be a healthy alternative to meat. However, some of his sanitarium patients had dental issues and couldn't chew the crunchy legumes. So, Dr. Kellogg ground the peanuts into a paste and called it "nut butter." On November 4, 1895, Dr. Kellogg filed a patent for a peanut-based "food compound."

However, according to the trade journal the *Peanut Promoter*, George A. Bayle was the first manufacturer of peanut butter, not Dr. Kellogg. Bayle opened a snack food company in 1888 with the unoriginal name of George A.

Bayle Company. He made and sold pretzels, Saratoga chip potatoes (if you remember, that was the name for potato chips), and salted peanuts. In 1894, Bayle tried grinding several products into pastes, including a cheese and nut paste similar to today's Cheez Whiz. Peanut butter was the only grinding experiment that stuck with his customers.

Another early contender for the first peanut butter maker was the Atlantic Peanut Refinery of Philadelphia, Pennsylvania. They were the first to use the words *peanut butter* on their jars and to receive an official trademark in 1898.

You might have heard that George Washington Carver invented peanut butter, but he couldn't have been the inventor because he was still in college when the first peanut butters hit the market. However, Carver *did* contribute a lot to peanut agriculture. After earning his master's degree in 1896, Carver taught agriculture at the Tuskegee Institute in Alabama. He encouraged farmers to alternate growing peanuts with growing cotton because the peanuts restored the nutrients to the soil after the cotton crops depleted it. To help make peanuts profitable for the farmers, he developed more than three hundred uses for peanuts and peanut oil, but that was after peanut butter had already been invented.

Another Fair Food

Yes, peanut butter was at the 1904 St. Louis World's Fair along with ice cream cones, hot dogs, and hamburgers. Even though peanut butter had been around for more than ten years before the fair opened, the exposure to hundreds of thousands of fairgoers helped boost its popularity. Food vender C. H. Sumner did really well selling peanut butter at the fair. He made a profit of $705, which would have been about $20,000 today.

The publicity from the fair helped peanut butter go national, and by 1910, every state had peanut butter manufacturers. Kansas had twenty-one different brands, if you can believe it! One reason there were so many different manufacturers was that peanut butter had to be sold locally before it spoiled. The oil in peanut butter would separate from the paste and sit on top. In three or four weeks, the peanut oil turned rancid. Since refrigerators didn't become common until the mid-1920s, people bought their peanut butter in small quantities from local vendors and ate it quickly before it went bad.

Two great minds solved the problem of peanut butter's oil separation at almost the same time. On March 17, 1921, Frank Stockton of Pittsburgh, Pennsylvania, filed a patent for full hydrogenation of peanut butter. Less than one month later, on April 5, 1921, Joseph Rosefield of Almeda, California, filed a patent for partial hydrogenation of peanut butter.

So, which peanut butter is better? Many would say that Rosefield's partially hydrogenated peanut butter was creamier than Stockton's fully hydrogenated peanut butter. After a few name changes and company buyouts, Rosefield's version eventually became Skippy and Stockton's version became Peter Pan.

HYDROGENATION

Warning: chemistry ahead!

Peanut oil stays liquid at room temperature because the molecules of peanut oil don't easily stack together. The molecules contain double bonds between carbon atoms, making them bent and kinked.

> The hydrogenation process bubbles hydrogen into the oil using a catalyst. The double bonds between carbons are replaced with single bonds between a carbon and a hydrogen; this makes the molecule flatter and able to stack together. This more compact structure means the oil is solid at room temperature.
>
> Full hydrogenation means that all the carbon atoms are bonded with hydrogen atoms. Partial hydrogenation means that some of the carbon atoms are bonded with hydrogen and some still have the double bonds.

About the same time as peanut butter got upgraded, one of the greatest things since sliced bread was invented. It was . . . sliced bread!

On the Way to PB&J

In 1912, Otto Frederick Rohwedder imagined how wonderful it would be if bread came presliced. After several years of trying, he came up with an automatic bread slicer. He paid a factory to build his machines, but before the first ones could be finished, a fire broke out, destroying his only set of blueprints and the model.

It took several years for him to save up enough money to try again. During that time, Otto talked to bakers and learned that they didn't like his idea at all. They thought the bread would go stale too quickly if it was presliced. So instead of that deterring him, Otto added an automatic wrapper to his new design as well.

After sixteen years of trying, Otto finally filed a patent application on November 26, 1928. In just a few short years, more than half the bread sold to customers came presliced. Otto's slicing machine revolutionized the baking industry and became the icon of innovation.

Other bakeries would refer to it when they wanted to announce new products. For example, in 1934, Bell Bakeries began printing a date on bread packages so customers would know it was fresh. The ad said, "This is the most progressive step that has been taken in the baking industry since sliced bread was introduced." An ad in 1939 for Rugers bakery's new loaf said, "It is the newest thing since sliced bread." The phrase eventually morphed into "The best thing since sliced bread" or "The greatest thing since sliced bread," which we still use today.

THE BEST THING

The Chillicothe Baking Company in Missouri sold the very first machine-sliced bread on July 6, 1928, using the automatic bread slicing machine invented by Otto Frederick Rohwedder. An article from the *Chillicothe Constitution-Tribune* described the event saying, "So neat and precise are the slices, so definitely better than anyone could possibly slice by hand with a bread knife that one realizes instantly that here is a refinement that will receive a hearty and permanent welcome." And it did receive a hearty and permanent welcome. Mothers loved sliced bread because now kids could make their own sandwiches. It also helped that the slices fit perfectly in the new pop-up toasters that had been invented a couple of years earlier.

By the 1930s, Americans had two of the three ingredients for the best sandwich ever, the PB&J. They had the peanut butter and they had sliced bread. But where was the jelly?

Jams and jellies have been around for a long time. For example, marmalade, which is made from oranges, has been around since the 1500s. It's not as if no one had thought of putting peanut butter with jelly. One of the earliest recipes was for peanut butter and crab apple jelly on bread, which appeared in the 1901 *Boston Cooking School Magazine of Culinary Science and Domestic Economics*. For some reason, it wasn't until the introduction of grape jelly during World War I that the idea of a peanut butter and jelly sandwich really took off.

The Welch family, creators of Concord grape juice, had been making unfermented grape juice since 1869. When they finally made their famous Concord grape juice into jelly, their entire first batch was bought by the US Army to be used for soldiers' rations during the war.

In WWII, peanut butter and grape jelly sandwiches were still part of the soldiers' field rations. Cheap, easy to make, and not needing refrigeration, PB&Js offered a good balance of protein, carbohydrates, and fat. Best of all, they tasted great. When the soldiers returned from the war, they continued to want PB&J sandwiches and they turned their kids onto them too. In no time, PB&Js filled lunch boxes all over America. And they still do.

Today, we use peanut butter in so many ways it's hard to count. Americans eat seven hundred million pounds of peanut butter a year, and it's estimated that 94 percent of American homes have a jar of peanut butter in the pantry at any given moment.

MAKING JELLY

A cool thing happens when you cook fruit juice and sugar together. The pectin, a polysaccharide found in the cell wall of plants, reacts with the sugar. As it cools, the pectin sets, making the fruit jellylike. The high heat also kills off microbes, so the jelly won't spoil even if not refrigerated.

PEANUT ALLERGIES

Reactions to a peanut allergy can range from an annoying rash to a deadly anaphylactic shock. New research suggests that peanut allergies have increased 21 percent since 2010 and doctors don't know why. It's not just peanuts, either; allergies to milk, eggs, shrimp, shellfish, and wheat have increased too.

Dr. John Harvey Kellogg was right: peanut butter is nutritious. The protein in peanuts is balanced with carbohydrates and mostly good fats. The list of nutrients includes vitamin E, folate, niacin, thiamine, riboflavin, vitamin B_6, zinc, copper, magnesium, phosphorus, potassium, calcium, and iron. They also contain resveratrol, which is believed to prevent heart disease, and beta-sitosterol, which has been shown to inhibit cancer growth.

Wow! You're probably thinking you should make yourself a PB&J right now! Slow down. Most of the major brands of peanut butter that we buy today also have added sugar, salt, and hydrogenated oil (a bad kind of fat), so that makes them a little less healthy. And when you read the ingredients of the most popular brands of jelly, you'll see sugar, high-fructose corn syrup, and corn syrup topping the list. That's a lot of sugar. If you want a superhealthy diet, stick with all-natural peanut butters and go easy on the jelly.

CHEW ON THIS!

* Arachibutyrophobia is the fear of peanut butter sticking to the roof of your mouth.
* Five hundred forty peanuts are used to make one 12-ounce jar of peanut butter.
* January 24 is National Peanut Butter Day.
* April 2 is National Peanut Butter and Jelly Day.
* Other names for the peanut include goober, groundnut, ground pea, earth-nut, pindar nut, and ground bean.
* Based on a survey by Peter Pan, Americans will eat nearly 3,000 PB&J sandwiches over the course of their lifetime.
* Former United States presidents Jimmy Carter and Thomas Jefferson were peanut farmers.

Second Helpings

Peanut butter is a natural for baking. Being sticky and oily makes it a great binder for other ingredients. In this cookie recipe, peanut butter replaces the flour completely, making this gluten-free as well. These will be the easiest cookies you've ever made and one of the yummiest.

EASY PEASEY PEANUT BUTTER COOKIES

Makes 1 dozen cookies

• **1 cup peanut butter**

• **1 cup sugar**

• **1 egg**

Preheat the oven to 350°F. Mix all the ingredients in a bowl until smooth. Put a tablespoon of batter on a cookie sheet. Flatten with a fork. Repeat to make eleven more cookies. Bake for 8 to 10 minutes, or until edges are slightly brown.

Chapter Eight

CUCKOO FOR COOKIES

COOKIES ARE AN INTEGRAL PART OF THE AMERICAN eating experience. Whether you're crowding around a flour-dusted table decorating holiday cookies, taking a plate of homemade cookies to a new neighbor, or buying them from a Girl Scout, these little baked sweets warm our hearts. And the warmest and most American of them all is the chocolate chip cookie.

Crispy on the outside and gooey in the middle, a fresh-out-of-the-oven chocolate chip cookie washed down with a glass of cold milk is what some people would describe as pure bliss. And the creator of this little bit of heaven was Ruth Wakefield. She made the very first chocolate chip cookie in 1938 at her restaurant—the Toll House—in Whitman, Massachusetts.

We know the who, the where, and the when of the chocolate chip cookie story, but do we know the how? Here are a couple of stories in American folklore. In the first story, Wakefield was making cookies but ran out of time to melt the chocolate before the dinner guests arrived. So, she chopped up a bar

of semisweet baking chocolate and dropped it into the batter. She assumed the chocolate would melt in the oven, but it didn't.

WHY DON'T CHOCOLATE CHIPS MELT?

It's not that chocolate chips don't melt when baked in a cookie; they do a little bit. You can see that when you pull apart a hot cookie. But semisweet chocolate (which is traditionally used in our favorite cookies) has less cocoa butter than milk chocolate, so it doesn't melt as easily. Also, the cookie dough helps support the shape of the chips until the cookie cools.

In another version of the story, Wakefield's mixer vibrated so much that it caused bits of chocolate to fall into the bowl from the shelf above. Having gone through the Great Depression, Wakefield didn't throw anything away and went ahead and baked the cookies with the chocolate bits included.

Both of those stories seem half-baked to the people who knew Ruth Wakefield. They described her as being a perfectionist, so those stories don't seem to fit her personality. She also frequently concocted new dishes and desserts. Therefore, the most likely story is that her "Toll House Chocolate Crunch Cookie" was just one of her many creations.

Her customers didn't care how Wakefield came up with chocolate chip cookies—they just wanted to eat them. After the Toll House cookie recipe came out in Wakefield's 1938 *Tried and True* cookbook, so many people began making them at home that stores had a hard time keeping semisweet chocolate bars in stock.

Nestlé executives noticed a spike in sales for their baking chocolate in New England. They sent a representative to investigate and found Ruth Wakefield and her recipe. Nestlé asked for Wakefield's permission to print the recipe on the package of its semisweet bars. She agreed for one dollar and a lifetime supply of chocolate.

Toward the end of 1939, Nestlé created grooves in their semisweet bar to make it easier to cut into 160 small pieces. Nestlé introduced chocolate chip morsels in 1940, but sugar shortages due to World War II halted production for several years, so they weren't commonly used until the mid-1950s.

Little did Wakefield know that her recipe would become one of America's most iconic desserts, inspiring hundreds if not thousands of other recipes and becoming the basis for many businesses, such as Mrs. Fields, Famous Amos, and Otis Spunkmeyer.

MASSACHUSETTS'S STATE COOKIE

On July 9, 1997, the chocolate chip cookie became the official state cookie of Massachusetts. Seems like a no-brainer since America's favorite cookie was invented there. However, the governor at the time was a big fan of the Fig Newton, which had also been created in Massachusetts. He wanted that to be the official state cookie. School children went to the governor's office and lobbied for the chocolate chip cookie instead, and they finally won. The Fig Newton got the consolation prize of being named the state's official *fruit* cookie.

Better Than a Biscuit

The way Americans went crazy for chocolate chip cookies, you'd think they'd never had a cookie before. But actually, humans have been baking small, sweet treats for as long as they were able to bake bread. The pharaohs in ancient Egypt ate cookielike snacks sweetened with honey. Around AD 600, the Persians figured out how to grow sugarcane and became the first people to make sugar cookies.

The first cookies in America came with the English and Dutch settlers in the early 1600s. The English called them *biscuits* while the Dutch called them *koekjes*, which means "little cake." That expression is believed to come from the practice of putting a small dollop of cake batter in the oven to test the temperature before baking the real cake.

In the 1700s, when the American colonists weren't getting along with the British very well, they chose to use the Dutch word *koekjes* instead of the British *biscuit*. They didn't want to use British words if they could help it. The American colonists spelled it either "cookie" or "cookey" because that's how it sounded to them.

DUTCH IMMIGRATION TO AMERICA

In 1609, Dutch immigrants settled around the Hudson River in what's current-day New York State. They named their colony New Netherlands. In 1626, Mayor Peter Minuit bought the island of Manhattan from the Native Americans for $24-worth of knives and beads. The Dutch built a town on the island and named it New Amsterdam. When the British barged in and took over the settlement in 1664, it was renamed New York.

Another wave of Dutch immigrants arrived in the 1800s. They came to America seeking better jobs and religious freedom. Nearly eighty million Americans have Dutch ancestry.

The Dutch have contributed many things to American culture, including bowling, crullers, and doughnuts (they called them *oliebollen*, but the American colonists called them doughnuts because they looked like walnuts. The holes came later).

Cookbooks from the 1700s and 1800s hold dozens of recipes for macaroons, gingersnaps, and shortbread cookies. Macaroons, in fact, are considered one of the oldest types of cookies. There are references in French texts to the *macaron* dating back to the early 1600s. When the cookie migrated to England, the word changed to "mackroon."

Gingersnaps were named for their extremely crunchy texture. When a person bit into a ginger cookie, it sounded like a stick snapping in two. And it's unclear whether shortbreads were called that because they are made with lots of "shortening" (another word for a fat, such as butter) or because an old Scottish definition of the word *short* meant "crumbly." Back in the 1700s, these cookies were also short on sugar. The Scottish version of shortbread used molasses as a sugar substitute, whereas the German version used honey.

It was common to use molasses or honey to sweeten baked goods in the seventeenth and eighteenth centuries, because granulated sugar was expensive and hard to get. Some cooks kept their meager supply of sugar locked in their spice cabinet to keep it safe from sneaky sweet-tooths. By the middle of the 1800s, new sugar-refining methods made it more affordable and it became more of a staple of cookie making.

WHY DID SUGAR USED TO BE SO EXPENSIVE?

In earlier days, sugarcane had to be harvested by hand and the sugarcane carefully separated from the green, leafy part of the plant. Once separated, workers squeezed out the juice from the cane, but there would always be bits of plant, dirt, or even bugs in the juice. To purify it, they added water and boiled it until the junky stuff rose to the top and could be skimmed off. Then, they boiled the juice some more until all the water had evaporated. That left wet crystallized sucrose, which was packed into clay jars to dry. Eventually, those blocks of sugar from the clay jars made it to colonial American cooks, who then had to grate it into a usable powder. It took a lot of work, so that's why sugar cost so much before production became industrialized. (Fun fact: Molasses is the thick brown syrup left-over after the sugar is refined.)

 # Cookies Go Commercial

Cookies have almost always been a homemade dessert because there wasn't a good way to keep them fresh while they sat on grocery store shelves. In 1899, the National Biscuit Company (later known as Nabisco) introduced a new package with an inner seal. This innovation allowed cookies to be mass-produced. Nabisco used its new packaging for animal crackers in 1902. The company's "Barnum's Animals" were cookies shaped like lions, tigers, bears, and other wild animals, in circus wagon–shaped boxes.

In 1908, the Loose-Wiles Biscuit Company released a cookie made with vanilla cream sandwiched between crunchy chocolate wafers. It was called the Hydrox. A fancy cookie, the Hydrox had a laurel wreath etched into the outer wafers. Like the Toll House cookie, the Hydrox went viral and was an absolute must-have at ice cream parlors. Later, the company name changed to Sunshine Biscuits because the owners, Jacob Loose and John Wiles, realized Loose-Wiles sounded like somebody with an honesty problem.

Nabisco wanted in on Hydrox's sweet success, so in 1912, it came out with its own crunchy chocolate sandwich cookie with vanilla cream filling. Nabisco called its version the Oreo. An obvious copy of the Hydrox, it even had a laurel wreath decoration!

It took more than forty years of superior advertising for Oreo to knock Hydrox off its cookie throne, but it finally did. Today, Oreos are the best-selling cookies in the world with more than 450 billion having been made since 1912.

WHERE DID THE NAME OREO COME FROM?

Nabisco has never explained how the Oreo cookie got its name, so lots of theories have been tossed around. One claims that the word "Oreo" is derived from the French word for "gold" because Oreos were first sold in gold packages. Another is that the two o's in the word represent the outer cookies while the *re* in the word *cream* goes in the middle, making an O-re-O. The cleverest theory, however, comes from Stella Parks in her book *Brave Tart: Iconic American Desserts*. She thinks Oreo comes from *Oreodaphne*, the Latin name for the mountain laurel used to decorate the wafers.

Cookies for a Good Cause

Competition in the snack food industry has always been intense. With so many choices on the grocery store shelves, it's a wonder that any company can stay afloat for long. Trying to compete with national, top-selling brands wouldn't normally be the best way to raise money. But that's exactly what the Mistletoe Girl Scout troop of Muskogee, Oklahoma, did in 1917. The scouts baked special cookies themselves and sold them at a high school auditorium and used the profit to pay for their troop's activities.

The idea spread among other troops, and in 1922, an article appeared in the Girl Scout magazine *The American Girl* with a sugar cookie recipe and a breakdown of the costs of ingredients. To ensure a profit, the suggested sales price was between 25 and 35 cents per dozen.

Eventually the amateur bakers couldn't keep up with demand for their cookies; after all, they were baking them in their own kitchens. In the 1930s, the Girl Scouts organization hired commercial bakers to make the cookies, so the girls could concentrate solely on selling them. Unfortunately, World War II forced them to halt cookie sales. During the war years, they sold calendars instead.

After the war, the Girl Scout cookie business picked up right where it had left off. In 1951, the scouts offered three kinds of cookies: a sandwich cookie, a shortbread, and a chocolate mint (which today we all know and love as Thin Mints).

Through the years, the Girl Scouts introduced other types of cookies to their roster. Some succeeded and some fell flat. The current best-selling Girl Scout cookies are Thin Mints, Samoas (also known as Caramel deLites), Tagalongs, S'Mores, and Do-si-dos. Each year approximately 2.3 million Girl Scouts sell nearly 200 million boxes of cookies.

If you're craving a Thin Mint in the middle of July, you'll have to wait. Girl Scout cookies are only sold January through April. But while you're waiting, you can bake a batch of Toll House cookies instead. They're easy to make—but don't forget the milk!

OH NO! NUTRITION

Cookies can be made more nutritious by adding healthy things to the batter, such as oatmeal and raisins for fiber, and peanut butter for protein. Fruit cookies, such as Fig Newtons, provide a few vitamins. But when you get right down to it, cookies are high in fat and sugar, which most Americans get too much of already.

The 2015-2020 edition of *Dietary Guidelines for Americans* recommends that added sugars make up less than 10 percent of the total calories consumed per day. If we use 2,000 calories a day as a base, that would mean you could have 200 calories of added sugar or 50 grams. Many food labels now include a line under "Total Carbohydrates" stating the amount of added sugars in grams, so peek at the ingredients list on your favorite cookie before eating too many!

CHEW ON THIS

* May 15 is National Chocolate Chip Cookie Day.
* June 12 is National Peanut Butter Cookie Day.
* Sesame Street's Cookie Monster first appeared in 1966.
* According to *Guinness World Records*, the biggest cookie weighed 40,000 pounds and was 102 feet wide. The Immaculate Baking Company made it on May 17, 2003, in Flat Rock, North Carolina, to raise money for the Folk Artist's Foundation. Read how they made it at www.immaculatebaking.com.
* China is the second-biggest market for Oreo cookies after the United States. The favorite Oreo flavor in China is Green Tea Ice Cream.
* Half of all Oreo eaters twist and pull apart their cookie before eating it. Women are more likely to do it than men.
* After 116 years, Nabisco uncaged Barnum's Animals. Since 2018, the animal cracker boxes include a zebra, a giraffe, a lion, a gorilla, and an elephant roaming free over the plains.

Second Helpings

Old recipes give us a glimpse of how hard it must have been to be a good baker. Check out this recipe for coconut macaroons as it appeared in *Mrs. Rorer's New Cook Book* printed in 1902. Notice the instruction to bake in a "slow oven." How would a cook know what that was? What if a cook accidently baked the cookies in a "medium oven"? For your information, a slow oven is 300° to 325°F.

COCONUT MACAROONS

Beat the whites of five eggs to a stiff froth; fold in carefully a half pound of powdered sugar sifted, and one and a half cups of grated or shredded coconut; stir very lightly. Drop by teaspoonsfuls on oiled paper, and bake in a slow oven twenty minutes. When done, take out of oven, and when cold, moisten the underside of the paper, and the macaroons may be easily loosened.

Chapter Nine

MUST . . . HAVE . . . CHOCOLATE

WHY DO PEOPLE LOVE CHOCOLATE SO MUCH? SIMPLE: because we're human! Our species is preprogrammed to love sweet foods and fatty foods, and chocolate is an irresistible combination of both.

Chocolate has been around for more than three thousand years, but it's a miracle that the ancient civilizations of Central America ever discovered it. Chocolate doesn't grow on trees, but the cacao seeds that make chocolate do. And you can't just pick a cacao seed and start eating it as you could an apple. Cacao seeds must go through several steps of processing before they can be used to make chocolate.

First, the seeds must ferment in a warm, dark place for a week; then they are dried in the sun for another week; and then roasted. Raw cacao seeds are so bitter that they're completely inedible. So, who figured this process out and gave us our beloved chocolate?

THE QUIRKY CACAO TREE

Cacao trees only grow within twenty degrees north or south longitude of the equator. They need steady, year-round rain to flourish. Even though these trees like a hot, damp climate, they can't handle direct sunlight so grow in the shade of taller trees.

It takes three to four years for a young tree to produce blossoms. The only way the blossoms can be pollinated are by tiny flies called midges. Out of one thousand flowers, only three or four will be pollinated and grow into seed pods. The pods take about six months to ripen—after all of that time, we finally get the cacao seeds and can start making chocolate.

According to Aztec legend, one of their many gods, Quetzalcoatl (ket-sahl-ko-AH-tul), came down to earth and taught people how to grow corn, how to work with silver, and how to turn the bitter cacao seeds into a thick, nutritious drink.

The drink, *cacahuatl* (ka-ka-wat-l), tasted nothing like our hot cocoa. The Aztecs liked it strong and bitter and seasoned with chile peppers. They believed cacahuatl made a person stronger and wiser. They also thought it was a love potion. Montezuma II, the last emperor of the Aztecs, drank it all day long, sometimes as many as forty cups a day!

The prized beverage made cacao beans so valuable that the Aztecs used them as money. Have you heard the saying, "Money doesn't grow on trees"? Well, it did for the Aztecs. However, the poor couldn't afford to drink cacahuatl. If a lowly laborer managed to get some beans, he used them to buy

other food. Three beans could get him an avocado; and thirty beans, a rabbit for his stew pot.

In 1519, the Spanish explorer Hernán Cortés discovered the Aztec empire and their gold and silver. Even though the fierce Aztecs were experienced warriors, their spears and battle axes were no match for Spanish guns. By 1521, Cortés had conquered the Aztecs and most of Mexico.

THE AZTEC EMPIRE, 1325–1522

The Aztec people settled in Mexico where Mexico City is now. They built the city of Tenochtitlán on an island in Lake Texcoco. By the time Cortés discovered it, more than 150,000 people lived there.

> The Aztecs were warriors and believed in human sacrifice. Despite their violent ways, they had an advanced culture with written language (hieroglyphics), art, mathematics, and an accurate calendar.

Cortés and his conquistadors tried cacahuatl while they were in Central America. They liked this invigorating energy drink, so they took it back to Spain with them. The Spanish made it better by adding sugar and leaving out the chile peppers. However, only Spanish nobility enjoyed the decadent drink because sugar and cacao beans were hard to get and very expensive.

POOP WATER?

The Aztecs called their drink *cacahuatl*, which meant "cacao water," but in Spanish, *caca* means "poop." It was embarrassing for the Spanish nobles to ask their servants to bring them poop water especially considering the drink was dark brown and thick. The Spanish started calling it *chocolatl*, which means "cocoa water." Later, English speakers changed it to *chocolate*.

Apparently, the rich and famous Spanish nobles wanted to keep the small supply of cacao beans to themselves because they didn't share their chocolate with the rest of Europe for nearly eighty years. Around 1600, news of the divine drink spread to mansions and palaces across Europe. By the 1700s, chocolate shops, kind of like today's Starbucks, sprouted up in England, France, Italy, and of course Spain.

Chocolate didn't take off in the American colonies, however, because it was insanely expensive to import from Europe. Then, in 1765, John Hannon, an Irish chocolate maker, and Dr. James Baker set up a trade route directly to the cacao plantations in the Caribbean. The Baker's Company still makes chocolate today, and, true to its name, it's used mainly for baking.

From Cup to Bar

The method for making chocolate hadn't changed much since the Aztecs' time. Cured cacao beans were ground into a paste and then stirred into water. But it never really did mix well with water. In 1828, the Dutch chemist Coenraad Van Houten solved that problem. He invented a press to squeeze out the fat from the cacao paste. That left a dry block that he crushed into a fine powder and added alkaline salts to. He called his new product "cocoa." (The rest of the world called it "Dutch cocoa.")

Van Houten's press opened the way for edible chocolate to be created. Up until then, it had always been mixed into a thick beverage that many people ate with a spoon. J. S. Fry & Sons, serving chocolate since 1728, made the first "eating" chocolate in 1847. The Frys took the extra cocoa butter—the fat squeezed out by Van Houten's press—and blended it with the Dutch cocoa powder and sugar. They molded that into a bar and called it "Chocolat Délicieux á Manger" (Delicious Chocolate to Eat) because it sounded better in French. Compared to our candy bars today, those early chocolate bars tasted terrible. But people had never had anything like it before and they wanted more.

Believe it or not, it took another twenty-eight years before milk chocolate was invented because chocolate makers had a chemical conundrum.

Chocolate contains a lot of oil and milk is mostly water. In case you didn't know, oil and water don't mix.

WHY OIL AND WATER DON'T MIX

Water is a polar liquid made up of a positively charged oxygen atom and negatively charged hydrogen atoms. When two water molecules meet up, the positive side of one is attracted to the negative side of the other and they bond.

Oil is a nonpolar liquid and it's attracted to other nonpolar liquids. When oil and water are combined, the water molecules stick to themselves and the oil molecules hang out together too.

Also, oil is less dense than water, so it floats on top, which makes mixing them even harder.

In 1875, Daniel Peter, a Swiss chocolate maker, teamed up with Henri Nestlé, a Swiss chemist. Nestlé had recently invented condensed milk and thought it might be the answer to creating a more delectable chocolate bar. The process required over a week of mixing to make one batch, but the sweet, creamy milk chocolate was worth it.

Other chocolate makers raced to imitate it, but Nestlé wouldn't share his secret. The others had to come up with their own recipes. Some of those early companies are still making chocolate today, such as Lindt, Cadbury, and Toblerone.

However, when most Americans think about chocolate, they think of two brands: Hershey's and Mars.

America's Chocolate

Before he molded his first candy bar, Milton Hershey had already become a millionaire selling caramels. Rich, happily married, and traveling around the world, Hershey had it all. Except . . . he was bored. Hershey had an inventive mind and he itched to do something new.

In 1893, Hershey went to the Columbian Exposition in Chicago and saw a thirty-eight-foot-tall statue made entirely of chocolate. The exhibit—by J. M. Lehmann Company from Germany—included a chocolate-making factory with everything from bean roasters to mixers. Hershey was so impressed that he bought the whole factory and had it shipped back to Lancaster, Pennsylvania.

Just like European chocolate makers, Hershey had to figure out his own recipe for milk chocolate. It took a few years, but finally, in 1900, he introduced the Hershey bar. He wanted everyone to enjoy chocolate, not just the wealthy, so he priced his candy bar at five cents. That price stayed the same for almost seventy years. How'd they do that? By shrinking the size of the bars. By 1967, they were about half the size of the originals.

Still experimenting and concocting, Hershey tried something different with his milk chocolate. Instead of pouring it into candy bar molds, he dropped it onto conveyor belts in little blobs. When the chocolate hit the belt, it made a smacking sound, like a kiss. Hershey's Kisses debuted in 1907 and Americans couldn't get enough of them.

MILTON HERSHEY (1857-1945)

In addition to being a wildly successful candy maker, Milton Hershey was incredibly generous. He built the whole town of Hershey, Pennsylvania, for his employees. Starting in 1903 with houses, parks, and schools, he later added a library, a post office, a theater, and a zoo.

In 1909, Hershey and his wife, Kitty, opened the Hershey Industrial School for orphan boys. After Kitty died, Hershey didn't care about money anymore since she wasn't around to share it with, so he donated his stock in the company to the school—a gift worth $60 million!

Other companies tried to replicate Hershey's success, but then America entered World War I in 1917 and that put a hold on candy inventions. After the war ended in 1918, Americans could afford candy again and the golden age of candy bars began. One of the stars of the candy bar golden age was Frank Mars, founder of the Mars Company. He introduced the Milky Way in 1924 and Snickers in 1930. Named after Frank's favorite horse, the Snickers bar is the best-selling candy bar in the world.

In 1940, Frank's son Forrest came up with an idea for a new chocolate candy coated with a colorful shell. The hard-candy shell kept the chocolate from melting, which was just what the United States military needed for its soldiers. In 1945, they bought millions of M&M's for soldiers' rations. But do you know what the M's stand for? It's for the original owners of the M&M's company: Forrest Mars and Bruce Murrie.

While Hershey's and Mars cornered most of the chocolate bar market, Otto Schnering, owner of the Curtiss Candy Company in Chicago, was also making a name for himself. In 1920, Schnering hired an airplane to fly over Pittsburgh doing stunts and drop Baby Ruth candy bars tied to little parachutes on the crowd of onlookers. It worked so well that he went on to do it in forty states. The Baby Ruth bar was a home run.

But this home run landed Schnering in court when he was sued by the real home run king, Babe Ruth. Schnering didn't have permission to use the baseball player's name, but he claimed that he named his candy bar after President Grover Cleveland's daughter Ruth—not the famous ballplayer. Everyone had a hard time believing that because Ruth had died of diphtheria seventeen years before the candy bar came out. But no one could prove that Schnering did *not* name it after her, so he won the court case.

Chocolate bars and chocolate companies have come and gone over the centuries since cacao beans arrived from Mexico. But one thing will never change: people love chocolate!

ON NO! NUTRITION

Good news! Chocolate contains flavanols, which some studies have shown to reduce heart disease. Chocolate also contains manganese, copper, magnesium, iron, calcium, potassium, and phosphorus. But before you eat a whole bag of chocolate candies, remember this one rule: the darker the chocolate the better. All the health benefits from chocolate can be achieved with one or two ounces of dark chocolate a day. Milk chocolate might satisfy your sweet tooth, but it won't do much to prevent heart attacks *and* it has a lot of unhealthy sugar.

Not only can chocolate keep your heart healthy, but it can also make you feel happier and more energetic. Phenylethylamine (PEA) and anandamide, two mood-enhancing chemicals associated with feelings of happiness, are found in chocolate. Chocolate's caffeine and theobromine help keep us alert and energetic. But if you really want to stay awake, chocolate won't do the job nearly as well as a can of cola. For instance, a Hershey candy bar has nine milligrams of caffeine compared with 33 milligrams in a 12-ounce soda.

CHEW ON THIS

* The Swedish scientist Carl von Linnaeus came up with the naming system for classifying living things. In 1753, he assigned the name *Theobroma cacao* to the cacao tree; it means "food of the gods."

* Every day, approximately 3,500,000 pounds of milk are used to make chocolate.

* The Swiss eat about 20 pounds of chocolate per person per year, which is more than any other country. Germany is second with 17 pounds; Ireland and the United Kingdom tie at third place with 16 pounds; and Americans are way down in ninth place at only 9½ pounds of chocolate a year.

* October 28 is National Chocolate Day.

* The Sperry Candy Company of Milwaukee, Wisconsin, introduced a chocolate bar in 1923 called Chicken Dinner, even though it didn't contain any chicken, just nuts and chocolate. The ads touted this candy bar as a wholesome meal. It was available in stores until 1962.

* Popular chocolate bars and the year they debuted:

Hershey bar 1900 • Goo Goo Clusters 1913 • Heath 1914 • Nestlé Crunch 1919 •

Baby Ruth 1920 • Mounds 1922 • Milky Way 1924 • Mr. Goodbar 1925 • Butterfinger 1928 •

Reese's Peanut Butter Cup 1928 • Snickers 1930 • 3 Musketeers 1932 • Fifth Avenue 1935

Second Helpings

The Aztecs didn't have access to sugar, so their cacahautl didn't taste anything like our hot chocolate. This recipe is similar to what the Aztecs drank.

AZTEC CACAHUATL

- **1 ounce unsweetened baking chocolate**
- **⅔ cup boiling water**
- **1 teaspoon vanilla extract**
- **¼ teaspoon chili powder**

Grate the chocolate as finely as possible. Put it into a bowl and add a little bit of boiling water. Mash the chocolate and water together to form a paste. Put the paste, the rest of the water, and the vanilla and chili powder in a blender and blend on high speed till it's frothy. Even after blending thoroughly, it will still have bits of chocolate floating in it and taste gritty.

NOTE: The Spanish had access to sugar. Their version of the drink was similar, but with sugar and cinnamon instead of the chili powder. You'll probably like the Spanish version better.

Chapter Ten
CEREAL WARS

I N 1894, DR. JOHN HARVEY KELLOGG AND WILL KEITH Kellogg developed the first ready-to-eat cereal, which eventually changed the way Americans started their day. But the Kellogg brothers couldn't agree if their cereal was a health food or a convenience food. The battle between the Kellogg brothers (and the birth of breakfast cereal) began in none other than Battle Creek, Michigan.

COOKED CEREALS

Although ready-to-eat cereals have only been around for about a century, humans have been cooking and eating cereals for thousands of years. Archaeologists discovered oat porridge in the stomach of a five-thousand-year-old human body in a peat bog in Europe.

Grains became an important part of the human diet approximately twelve thousand years ago, when rice was domesticated in China. Europe started growing rye and oats about ten thousand years ago and then, later, wheat and barley.

Before the Kelloggs created cold cereals, Americans tended to eat large, meat-based breakfasts. Bacon and eggs were standard in the mid-1800s, but breakfast might also include fried potatoes, fish, fruit, and biscuits. Cereals were always cooked, sometimes for hours, into thick porridges. It wasn't just at breakfast that Americans ate a lot of meat and pork, though. The general diet of the day was heavy on beef and light on fruits and vegetables.

Because of the heavy, hard-to-digest meals, people tended to suffer from stomach ailments. Abdominal pain, heartburn, constipation, gas, and bloating were symptoms of dyspepsia. To get relief, and hopefully get well, some sufferers went to fancy health spas called sanitariums.

In 1878, Dr. Kellogg opened the Battle Creek Sanitarium. His younger brother, Will Keith, joined him in 1880 to manage their side business, the Sanitas Food Company. The Kellogg brothers were Seventh-day Adventists and followed the teachings of James Caleb Jackson, one of the early members of the church. Jackson advocated for Clean Living, a lifestyle that included a vegetarian diet, exercise, and an avoidance of sugar, caffeine, alcohol, and tobacco.

SEVENTH-DAY ADVENTISTS

Officially established in Battle Creek, Michigan, in 1863, this Christian protestant church began with 3,500 members and has grown to nineteen million followers.

Seventh-day Adventists have twenty-eight fundamental beliefs, and one is that their bodies are temples of the Holy Spirit and should be cared for with adequate exercise, rest, and a healthy diet. Many follow plant-based diets and abstain from tobacco, alcohol, and narcotics. As their name implies, they go to church on Saturdays, the seventh day of the week.

To improve their patients' diets, the Kellogg brothers experimented with new vegetarian foods (including peanut butter, discussed in Chapter 7). They were interested in cereals because they thought they would help alleviate chronic constipation. Dr. Kellogg had wanted to develop a ready-to-eat cereal since his college days, where he got the idea when he was a poor student living in a cheap boardinghouse. He didn't have access to a kitchen to cook oatmeal and wished he could eat it right out of a box.

The Kelloggs weren't the first ones to try cold cereals, however. Their mentor, James Caleb Jackson, had already invented a breakfast cereal at his sanitarium in Danville, New York, in 1863. He called his nuggets of graham flour "Granula." The clumps of ground-up, baked grain had to be softened by soaking them all night in water; otherwise, they might crack a tooth. And they tasted like cardboard. Needless to say, Granula wasn't a big hit. One of the Kelloggs' early attempts at cereal, "Granola," was eerily like Jackson's Granula. Theirs tasted bad too.

In 1894, the Kellogg brothers accidently got their big break. They had made a batch of wheat dough and left it sitting on the counter overnight. When they went back the next day, the dried-out dough was stale. Always frugal, they put it through the rollers anyway, but instead of coming out flat, it crumbled into flakes. The brothers went ahead and baked the flakes to see what would happen. A tasty, crunchy (but not too crunchy) wheat flake came out of the oven—and it tasted good!

Dr. Kellogg applied for a patent on "Flaked Cereal and Process of Preparing the Same" on May 31, 1895. Then, the Kelloggs started selling their wheat flakes to their patients at the San (the nickname of the Battle Creek Sanitarium).

The Brothers' Battle Begins

While Dr. Kellogg concentrated on his busy medical practice, Will Keith perfected the cereal flake recipe. He discovered that corn worked better than wheat. He also discovered that if he added sugar, the flakes stayed fresher longer and tasted better.

Will Keith knew everyone would love this cereal if they only knew about it. He wanted to expand the marketing for it and to promote it as a tasty, convenient breakfast food—not just a high-fiber health food for the patients at the sanitarium.

Dr. Kellogg, however, threw a fit. He had spent his career trying to get people to quit eating sugar and was furious that his brother had added sugar to their cereal. Dr. Kellogg cared much more about his reputation as a physician than he cared about making money. The addition of sugar also went against his beliefs as a devout Seventh-day Adventist.

Will Keith saw potential in the cornflakes and pressed on with his plan. In 1906, after twenty-five years of working for his big brother, Will Keith quit his job at the San and opened the Battle Creek Toasted Corn Flake Company. Later, he changed the name of the company to Kellogg's. That ticked off Dr. Kellogg so much that he sued his brother. Will Keith sued him back. For the next twenty years, the two brothers barely spoke to each other except in the courtroom.

WILL KEITH KELLOGG (1860–1951)

A brilliant businessman, Will Keith understood the value of advertising and maintaining quality. By 1925, after only being open for nineteen years, the Kellogg's Company had made him a multimillionaire.

Will Keith gave back to his community by building a recreation center, a school, and an auditorium in Battle Creek. He also established the Kellogg Foundation in 1930 to promote health and education for children.

During the Great Depression, many companies laid off workers, but not Will Keith Kellogg. Instead of two eight-hour shifts, he switched to three six-hour shifts so more people could have a job. A smaller paycheck was better than no paycheck when 25 percent of Americans were out of work.

Competition Moves In

As if having his brother mad at him wasn't enough, Will Keith had another problem. He'd been pirated.

In 1891, C. W. Post went to the Battle Creek Sanitarium hoping to cure his serious digestion problems. To help pay his medical bills, he worked with Will Keith in the experimental kitchen during the development of some of their food products. In 1892, Post shocked the Kellogg brothers by opening his own sanitarium in Battle Creek as well as his own health food business. In 1895, he started selling Grape-Nuts, which were almost identical to the Kelloggs' Granola except they tasted better.

Post started selling Post Toasties in 1904, an almost exact copy of Kellogg's cornflakes. A feud between the two companies escalated into an all-out advertising war. Unfortunately, Post wasn't the only copycat. By 1911, 107 brands of cornflakes were being made in Battle Creek alone.

Meanwhile, in Bedford Park, New York, in 1901, a botanist working for the newly formed New York Botanical Gardens made an explosive discovery. Alexander Pierce Anderson was testing a theory that all grains contained a small amount of condensed water and that, when heated, they would explode like popcorn. He put wheat and rice in sealed glass tubes and heated the tubes.

When he thought they were hot enough, he cracked them with a hammer. It sounded like a shotgun. When the grains exploded out of the tubes, they were puffed like popcorn.

Anderson realized this discovery might be the next great food sensation. He quit his job as a botanist and started working on the patent. He sold his patented process to Quaker Oats Company and they introduced Puffed Rice cereal in 1905.

"PUFFED RICE, THE CEREAL SHOT FROM A CANNON."

That was the slogan of one of the most exciting food exhibits at the 1904 St. Louis World's Fair. Anderson Puffed Rice Company used cannons from the Spanish-American War to shoot the rice. Once an hour, the cannons were heated up until the rice exploded out of them. Freshly puffed rice was coated in caramel and sold by the bagful to fairgoers.

Even with patents protecting the manufacturing process of these cereals, other companies could get around each patent by changing one little thing in their cereals, such as adding an ingredient or using a different machine to produce the food. They constantly stole one another's ideas. Even the Kellogg's Company was at fault. It came out with its own puffed cereals, Rice Krispies, in 1927; Corn Pops, in 1950; and Honey Smacks (originally called Sugar Smacks), in 1953. General Mills—another food production company—introduced its puffed corn cereal Kix in 1937. Then, General Mills hit the jackpot in 1941 with its puffed oat cereal Cheerios (originally called CheeriOats), which is still the best-selling brand of cereal in America.

Advertising Wars

Advertising made all the difference when it came to which cereal companies flourished and which floundered. Will Keith Kellogg and C. W. Post were brilliant marketers. Post was the first to offer a prize in a cereal box when he included a booklet, *The Road to Wellville*, in each box of Grape-Nuts. Will Keith Kellogg advertised directly to kids by printing a mail-in coupon on the cornflakes box in 1909. If kids mailed the coupon to Kellogg's, they would get a *Kellogg's Funny Jungleland Moving-Pictures* book sent to them.

After World War II, the manufacturing of plastic toys became cheap and companies began putting toys inside cereal boxes. One of the most popular cereal toys came out in 1955 in Kellogg's Corn Flakes and Frosted Flakes. These tiny plastic scuba diving figures, called Frogmen, would swim and dive in the bathtub after baking soda had been placed on their feet.

In addition to putting toys in cereals to attract young shoppers, cereal companies advertised on popular children's television and radio shows. Kellogg's went a step further and created characters for their cereals. The three elves Snap, Crackle, and Pop debuted in 1928 with the new cereal Rice Krispies, and Tony the Tiger came out in 1952 with Frosted Flakes cereal.

It wasn't just great advertising that helped make breakfast cereals a fixture in American homes. Milk had also become better and safer to consume. Advancements in pasteurization, refrigeration, and packaging meant there was plenty of cold milk for kids to pour on their cornflakes.

Moms were thrilled with cereals. No more frying eggs or flipping pancakes every morning. Kids could make their own breakfast now and clean up after themselves too.

FORTIFIED CEREALS

Vitamin deficiencies were common in children, especially during the Great Depression. Rickets, a deficiency of vitamin D, caused weak, soft bones and skeletal deformities. Pellagra, a deficiency of niacin (vitamin B_3), caused diarrhea, dementia, and rashes. Pellagra could be fatal if left untreated.

In the 1930s, the American Medical Association and the United States Food and Drug Administration encouraged cereal manufacturers to add niacin, iron, riboflavin, and thiamine to their cereals. Calcium and vitamin D were added in the 1940s.

Rickets and pellagra are extremely rare now, partly due to breakfast cereals.

Kids Versus Parents

Unfortunately, as the battle for kid customers heated up, companies added more and more sugar to their cereals. By the mid-1950s, some of the most popular ready-to-eat cereals contained as much as 45 percent sugar. In the 1970s, these high-sugar products were blamed for the rise in obesity in America's children. A wave of healthier cereals started hitting the market shortly after that. Although the kids begged for the sugary cereal with the new collectable toy, parents started buying the bland, boring boxes of healthy whole grains. This battle continues to be fought in grocery aisles all over America to this day.

Cereal started out as a health food, then went to sugar's unhealthy dark side. We can only imagine that Dr. John Harvey Kellogg is somewhere saying, "I told you so."

Made with whole grains, fortified with vitamins and minerals, and served with milk, a bowl of cereal could be a healthy part of your daily diet, providing fiber, carbohydrates, and essential vitamins. But it might also have too much added sugar. The current dietary guidelines recommend no more than 10 percent of your daily calories should come from sugar. You're going to have to read the labels to find out which cereals would be a healthy part of your daily diet and which ones should be considered a special and occasional treat.

CHEW ON THIS

* More than 128 billion bowls of Corn Flakes are eaten each year.
* The number-one-selling cereal in the United States in 2018 was Cheerios, followed by Honey Nut Cheerios.
* Of the $8.5 billion in cereal sales each year, Kellogg's, Post, General Mills, and Quaker Foods are responsible for $7.3 billion of that.
* In 1955, Quaker Puffed Rice cereal included a deed of land in each box for "one square inch of Yukon land." Quaker sold more than 21 million boxes of cereal that year. It's a shame those deeds are worthless now. It seems the Quaker company forgot to pay the property taxes of $37.20 and the Canadian government confiscated the land.
* National Cereal Day is March 7.
* A cereal is a type of grass and the grain is botanically considered to be a type of fruit called a caryopsis.
* On December 24, 1926, the first singing radio commercial aired and it was for Wheaties, which had been introduced by General Mills in 1921.

Second Helpings

Breakfast cereals are fortified with many essential vitamins and minerals including iron. This magnetic metal is vital to our health. It's in our hemoglobin, a part of our red blood cells, and without iron, our red blood cells can't carry oxygen as needed. Having low iron is called being anemic.

You can do this simple experiment to actually see the iron that is included in your cereal.

EXTRACTING IRON FROM BREAKFAST CEREAL

YOU'LL NEED:

- ½ cup of fortified cereal (simple cereals work best, such as Cheerios or Chex)
- Bowl
- Spoon or ladle
- Piece of white paper
- Strong magnet

1. Crush the cereal in the bowl with the spoon or the back of a ladle. Keep crushing until it's a fine powder.

2. Spread the powder in a thin layer across the white paper.

3. Without touching the powder, pass the magnet as close to the cereal as you can.

4. Look at the magnet. You should be able to see tiny specks stuck to it. That's the iron. If you didn't get anything, try a stronger magnet.

Selected Sources

Finding all the fun stories and fascinating facts about our favorite foods required a lot of sources including printed books, ebooks, internet articles, websites, and blog posts. I don't want to bore you with that very, very long list, so I've selected the most important sources for each chapter.

CHAPTER ONE
There's No Ham in Hamburgers

2015–2020 Edition of the Dietary Guidelines for Americans. United States Department of Health and Human Services. https://health.gov/dietaryguidelines/2015/guidelines.

"Early American Cookbooks." Hathi Trust. https://babel.hathitrust.org/cgi/mb?a=listis&c=1934413200.

Edge, John T. *Hamburger and Fries: An American Story.* New York: G. P. Putnam's Sons, 2005.

"Genghis Khan." History. www.history.com/topics/china/genghis-khan. A & E Television.

Love, John F. *McDonald's: Behind the Arches.* New York: Bantam Books, 1995.

Rozin, Elizabeth. *The Primal Cheeseburger: A Generous Helping of Food History Served up on a Bun.* New York: Penguin Books, 1994.

Tannahill, Reay. *Food in History.* New York: Crown Publishers, Inc., 1988.

Vaccaro, Pamela. *Beyond the Ice Cream Cone: The Whole Scoop on Food at the 1904 World's Fair.* St. Louis: Enid Press, 2004.

"World Records." *Guinness World Records.* www.guinnessworldrecords.com.

Zimmer, Carl. *Microcosm: E. coli and the New Science of Life.* New York: Pantheon Books, 2008.

CHAPTER TWO
One Potato, Two Potato

Burhans, Dirk. *Crunch! A History of the Great American Potato Chip.* Madison: University of Wisconsin Press, 2017.

"The Columbian Exchange: An Overview." Scholastic. Accessed June 20, 2019. www.scholastic.com/teachers/articles/teaching-content/columbian-exchange-overview/.

"Early American Cookbooks." Hathi Trust. https://babel.hathitrust.org/cgi/mb?a=listis&c=1934413200.

Edge, John T. *Hamburger and Fries: An American Story.* New York: G. P. Putnam's Sons, 2005.

Haber, Barbara. *From Hardtack to Home Fries: An Uncommon History of American Cooks and Meals.* New York: Free Press, 2002.

Kelly, John. *The Graves Are Walking: The Great Famine and the Saga of the Irish People.* New York: Henry Holt & Company, 2012.

Love, John F. *McDonald's: Behind the Arches.* New York: Bantam Books, 1995.

Mann, Charles C. "How the Potato Changed the World." *Smithsonian Magazine,* November 2011. www.smithsonianmag.com/history/how-the-potato-changed-the-world-108470605.

"Mr. Potato Head." Toy Hall of Fame. www.toyhalloffame.org.

Raj, Ajai. "Here's Why Stale Bread Is Hard, but Stale Chips Are Soft." *Business Insider,* September 7, 2014. https://www.businessinsider.com/what-makes-bread-and-chips-stale-2014-9.

Rozin, Elizabeth. *The Primal Cheeseburger: A Generous Helping of Food History Served up on a Bun.* New York: Penguin Books, 1994.

Schlosser, Eric. *Fast Food Nation: The Dark Side of the All-American Meal.* New York: Houghton Mifflin Company, 2002.

Tannahill, Reay. *Food in History.* New York: Crown Publishers, Inc., 1988.

CHAPTER THREE
Eatsa Some Pizza

Barrett, Liz. *Pizza: A Slice of American History.* Minneapolis: Voyager Press, 2014.

Bernstein, Lenny. "We Eat 100 Acres of Pizza a Day." *Washington Post,* January, 20, 2015. www.washingtonpost.com/news/to-your-health/wp/2015/01/20/we-eat-100-acres-of-pizza-a-day.

"Clarence Birdseye." Famous Scientists. www.famousscientists.org/clarence-birdseye.

Gelbert, Doug. *So Who the Heck Was Oscar Mayer: The Real People Behind Those Brand Names.* New York: Barricade Books, 1996.

Helstosky, Carol. *Pizza: A Global History.* London: Reaktion Books, Ltd., 2008.

"History of Cheese." International Dairy Foods Association. www.idfa.org/news-view/media-kits/cheese.

"Italian Immigration." Library of Congress. www.loc.gov/teachers/classroommaterials/presentationsandactivities/presentations/immigration/italian3.html.

Mariani, John F. *How Italian Food Conquered the World.* New York: Palgrave Macmillan, 2011.

"The Method of Making a Frozen Pizza." Google Patents. Patents.google.com/patent/US2668117A/en.

CHAPTER FOUR
We All Scream for Ice Cream

"About the White House." White House. www.whitehouse.gov/about-the-white-house/the-white-house/.

Arnold, Shannon Jackson. *Everybody Loves Ice Cream: The Whole Scoop on America's Favorite Treat.* Cincinnati: Emmis Books, 2004.

Busenberg, Bonnie. *Vanilla, Chocolate, & Strawberry: The Story of Your Favorite Flavors.* Minneapolis: Lerner Publications, 1994.

Butler, Orville R. *From Ice House to Refrigerator.* Ultimate History Project. www.ultimatehistoryproject.com/ice-house.html.

"Ice Cream." Thomas Jefferson's Monticello. www.monticello.org/site/research-and-collections/ice-cream.

"Ice Cream in a Bag." Oregon State College of Engineering, July 2004. https://engineering.oregonstate.edu/momentum/k12/july04/index.html.

"Our Story." Menches Brothers. www.menchesbros.com.

Rain, Patricia. *Vanilla: The Cultural History of the World's Favorite Flavor and Fragrance.* New York: Penguin Group, 2004.

Root, Waverly, and Richard de Rochement. *Eating in America: A History.* New York: The Echo Press, 1976.

Scofield, Merry Ellen. *Unraveling the Dolley Myths.* White House Historical Association. Whitehousehistory.org/unraveling-the-dolley-myths.

Strom, Caleb. *Ancient Advanced Technology: 2,400-Year-Old Yakhchals Kept Ice in the Desert.* Ancient Origins, November 6, 2017. Ancient-origins.net/artifacts-ancient-technology/ancient-technology-2400-year-old-yakhchals-kept-ice-desert-021700.

Tannahill, Reay. *Food in History.* New York: Crown Publishers, Inc., 1988.

Theobald, Mary Miley. "Some Cold Hard Historical Facts about Good Old Ice Cream." *Colonial Williamsburg Journal*, Spring 2010. www.history.org/foundation/journal/spring10/icecream.cfm.

Vaccaro, Pamela. *Beyond the Ice Cream Cone: The Whole Scoop on Food at the 1904 World's Fair.* St. Louis: Enid Press, 2004.

CHAPTER FIVE

A Hot Dog by Any Other Name

"British Royal Visit." Franklin D. Roosevelt Presidential Library and Museum. www.fdrlibrary.org/royal-visit.

"Dachshund." American Kennel Club. www.akc.org/dog-breeds/dachshund.

"FAQ: Processed Meat and Cancer." American Institute for Cancer Research, August 7, 2014. www.aicr.org/enews/2014/08-august/faq-processed-meat-and-html.

Gelbert, Doug. *So Who the Heck Was Oscar Mayer: The Real People Behind Those Brand Names.* New York: Barricade Books, 1996.

Hippisley Coxe, Antony and Araminta. *The Great Book of Sausages.* Woodstock, NY: The Overlook Press, 1996.

"Hot Dog Eating Contest." Nathan's Famous. https://nathansfamous.com/hot-dog-eating-contest.

"Hot Dogs and Food Safety." United States Department of Agriculture, Food Safety and Inspection Service, updated August 6, 2013. https://www.fsis.usda.gov/wps/portal/fsis/topics/food-safety-education/get-answers/food-safety-fact-sheets/meat-preparation/hot-dogs-and-food-safety/CT_Index.

"How Hot Dogs Are Made." National Hot Dog and Sausage Council. www.hot-dog.org/culture/
         hot-hot-dogs-are-made/.

Kraig, Bruce and Patty Carroll. *Man Bites Dog: Hot Dog Culture in America.* Lanham, MD: Taylor Trade
         Publishing, 2012.

"Mustard." *Encyclopaedia Britannica,* February 25, 2019. www.britannica.com/plant/mustard.

"Our Story." McCormick-French's. www.mccormick.com/frenchs/story.

Shephard, Sue. *Pickled, Potted, and Canned: How the Preservation of Food Changed Civilization.* London:
         Headline Book Publishing, 2000.

Tannahill, Reay. *Food in History.* New York: Crown Publishers, Inc., 1988.

"Thomas Aloysius Dorgan." *Encyclopaedia Britannica,* last updated April 28, 2019. https://Britannica.com/
         biography/Thomas-Aloysius-Dorgan.

Vaccaro, Pamela. *Beyond the Ice Cream Cone: The Whole Scoop on Food at the 1904 World's Fair.* St. Louis:
         Enid Press, 2004.

Vyas, Kashyap. "19 Greatest Inventions of the Roman Empire That Helped Shape the Modern World."
         Interesting Engineering, March 6, 2018. www.interestingengineering.com/19-greatest-inventions-
         of-the-roman-empire-that-helped-shape-the-modern-world.

CHAPTER SIX

Chickens Don't Have Fingers

Barth, Brian. "How to Incubate Chicken Eggs." Modern Farmer. www.Modernfarmer.com/2015/04/how-to-
         incubate-chicken-eggs.

"Colonel Harland Sanders Biography." Biography, April 27, 2017; updated October 18, 2019. www.biography.
         com/buisness-figure/colonel-harland-sanders/.

Cowart, Leigh. "The Weird History of Vitamin D and What It Actually Has to Do with the Sun." *Washington
         Post,* May 12, 2016. https://www.washingtonpost.com/news/speaking-of-science/wp/2016/05/12/
         the-weird-history-of-vitamin-d-and-what-it-actually-has-to-do-with-sun/?noredirect=on.

DeLuca, Hector F. "History of the Discovery of Vitamin D and Its Active Metabolites." National Library of
         Medicine, January 8, 2014. ncbi.nlm.nih.gov/pmc/articles/PMC3899558/.

Edge, John T. *Fried Chicken: An American Story.* New York: G. P. Putnam's Sons, 2004.

"Guthrie's—About Us." Guthrie's Chicken. Guthrieschicken.com/about-us/.

Heitz, Kelly. "The Story of the Chicken Finger." *South Magazine,* April 1, 2016. Southmag.com/April-
         May-2016/The-story-of-the-chicken-finger/.

"History of the American Heart Association." American Heart Association. www.heart.org/-/media/files/
         about-us/history/.

"How Spanky's Original Chicken Finger Was Invented." Spankysriverstreet.com/about-us/.

Lawler, Andrew. *Why Did the Chicken Cross the World?: The Epic Saga of the Bird That Powers Civilization.* New York: Atria Books, 2014.

Lawler, Andrew, and Jerry Adler. "How the Chicken Conquered the World: The Epic Began in Asia 10,000 Years Ago and Ended Up in Kitchens All over the World." *Smithsonian Magazine,* June 2012. Smithsonianmag.com/history/how-the-chicken-conquered-the-world-87583657/.

Love, John F. *McDonald's: Behind the Arches.* New York: Bantam Books, 1995.

Pollan, Michael, adapted by Richie Chevat. *The Omnivore's Dilemma: The Secrets Behind What You Eat.* New York: Dial Books for Young Readers, 2009.

Powell, Hugh. "T. Rex Linked to Chickens, Ostriches." *Smithsonian Magazine,* April 24, 2008. Smithsonianmag.com/science-native/t-rex-linked-to-chickens-ostriches-180940877/.

Rude, Emelyn. "Secrets of the Chicken Nugget: A Surprising History." *Time,* August 2, 2016. https://time.com/4431334/history-chicken-nuggets/.

Rude, Emelyn. *Tastes Like Chicken: A History of America's Favorite Bird.* New York: Pegasus Books, 2017.

"Why Did They Call Them Chicken Fingers?" Email interview with Katie Murphy of Live Oak Restaurant Group, November 21, 2019.

CHAPTER SEVEN
Peanut Butter Better

"17 Fun Facts About Peanuts and Peanut Butter." National Peanut Board. Accessed July 29, 2019. www.nationalpeanutboard.org/peanut-info/fun-facts.htm.

Gillies, Trent. "Why Peanut Reactions Have Become 'Almost Epidemic' and What to Do About Food Allergies." CNBC, October 28, 2018. www.cnbc.com/2018/10/26/why-peanut-food-allergies-have-become-almost-epidemic-html.

"The History." Concord Grape Association. www.concordgrape.org/bodyhistory.html.

Krampner, Jon. *Creamy and Crunchy: An Informational History of Peanut Butter, The All-American Food.* New York: Columbia University Press, 2013.

Markel, Howard. *The Kelloggs: The Battling Brothers of Battle Creek.* New York: Pantheon Books, 2017.

"New Study Suggests 21 % Increase in Childhood Peanut Allergy Since 2010." American College of Allergy, Asthma, and Immunology, October 27, 2017. https://acaai.org/news/new-study-suggests-21- percent-increase-childhood-peanut-allergy-2010.

Nix, Elizabeth. "Who Invented Sliced Bread?" History, last updated August 22, 2018. Accessed July 22, 2019. www.history.com/news/who-invented-sliced-bread.

"Otto Frederick Rohwedder." Lemelson-MIT. https://lemelson.mit.edu/resources/otto-frederick-rohwedder.

"Peanut Nutrition Data." The Peanut Institute. https://peanut-institute.com/peanut-facts/nutritional-breakdown/#nutritional/3.

Smith, Andrew F. *Peanuts: The Illustrious History of the Goober Pea.* Urbana: University of Illinois Press, 2012.

"Who Invented the Peanut Butter and Jelly Sandwich?" National Peanut Board. www.nationalpeanutboard.org/news/who-invented-the-peanut-butter-and-jelly-sandwich.htm.

CHAPTER EIGHT

Cuckoo for Cookies

"Cookie History." Girl Scouts. www.girlscouts.org/en/cookies/all-about-cookies/cookie-history.html.

"Dutch Immigration." Spartacus Educational. https://spartacus-educational.com/USAEHolland.htm.

"Early American Cookbooks." Hathi Trust. https://babel.hathitrust.org/cgi/mb?a=listis&c=1934413200.

"History of Sugar." The Sugar Association. www.sugar.org/sugar/history.

Meyer, Ziati. "Nabisco Uncages Its Animal Crackers After 116 Years." *USA Today,* August 21, 2018. https://www.usatoday.com/story/money/2018/08/21/nabisco-uncages-its-animal-crackers-after-116-years/989928002/.

Michaud, Jon. "Sweet Morsels: A History of the Chocolate-Chip Cookie." *New Yorker,* December 22, 2013. https://www.newyorker.com/culture/culture-desk/sweet-morsels-a-history-of-the-chocolate-chip-cookie.

Parks, Stella. "How Oreos Got Their Name: The Rise of an American Icon." *Serious Eats,* August 15, 2017. www.seriouseats.com/2017/08/print/history-of-oreos-bravetart-cookbook.html.

Wyman, Carolyn. *The Great American Chocolate Chip Cookie Book.* Woodstock, VT: The Countryman Press, 2014.

CHAPTER NINE

Must . . . Have . . . Chocolate

Brenner, Joel Glenn. *The Emperors of Chocolate: Inside the Secret World of Hershey and Mars.* New York: Random House, 1999.

Coe, Sophie D., and Michael D. Coe. *The True History of Chocolate.* London: Thames and Hudson, 1996.

Gottlieb, Bill. *Good News! Even More Health Benefits from Dark Chocolate. Bottom Line Personal,* April 15, 2015.

Helmenstine, Anne Marie. "Why Oil and Water Don't Mix." Thought Company, updated July 5, 2018. www.thoughtco.com/why-oil-and-water-dont-mix-609193.

Mikkelson, David. "Was the Baby Ruth Named After Ruth Cleveland?" Snopes, updated May 31, 2011. www.snopes.com/business/names/babyruth.asp.

"Pollinators: Chocolate Midges." U.S. National Park Service, updated February 13, 2015. www.nps.gov/articles/chocolate-midge.htm.

Trager, James. *The Food Chronology: A Food Lover's Compendium of Events and Anecdotes from Prehistory to the Present.* New York: Henry Holt & Company, 1995.

Wells, Jeff. "Clucking Sweet History: A Candy Bar Called Chicken Dinner." Mental Floss, November 2, 2015. www.mentalfloss.com/article/70510/clucking-sweet-history-candy-bar-called-chicken-dinner.

CHAPTER TEN
Cereal Wars

Anderson, Heather Arndt. *Breakfast: A History.* Lanham, MD: Rowman & Littlefield, 2013.

Burrows, Dan. "America's Most Popular Breakfast Cereals (And the Stocks Behind Them)." Kiplinger, October 11, 2018. www.kiplinger.com/slideshow/investing/T052-5001-america-s-most-popular-breakfast-cereals-stocks/index.html.

Casanova, Amanda. "10 Things Everyone Should Know About Seventh-Day Adventists and Their Beliefs." *Christianity Today,* April 13, 2018. www.christianity.com/church/denomination/10-things-everyone-should-know-about-seventh-day-adventists-and-their-beliefs.html.

Chavey, Eddy. "50 Greatest Cereal Box Prizes." Mr. Breakfast. www.mrbreakfast.com/list.asp?id=6.

Harmen, Katherine. "Get the Iron Out of Your Breakfast Cereal." *Scientific American,* May 20, 2011. www.scientficamerican.com/article/get-the-iron-out-of-your-breakfast-cereal-bring-science-home/.

"Kellogg Company: A Historical Overview." Kellogg Company. www.kellogghistory.com/history/html.

Markel, Howard. *The Kelloggs: The Battling Brothers of Battle Creek.* New York: Pantheon Books, 2017.

Vaccaro, Pamela. *Beyond the Ice Cream Cone: The Whole Scoop on Food at the 1904 World's Fair.* St. Louis: Enid Press, 2004.

Vargues, Lisa. "Breakfast in a Blast: The Invention of Puffed Cereal at NYBG." New York Botanical Gardens, May 8, 2015. www.nybg.org/blogs/science-talk/2015/05/breakfast-in-a-blast-the-invention-of-puffed-cereal-at-nybg.

Acknowledgments

Getting the idea for this book was easy. Getting that idea actually *made* into a book required the knowledge, skill, and support of a lot of people. First, I want to thank my amazing agent, John Rudolph of Dystel, Goderich & Bourret, LLC. He saw promise in my proposal and found the perfect home for it at Running Press Kids. My editors Allison Cohen and Julie Matysik have been wonderful to work with and they had the insight to get Peter Donnelly to illustrate. I couldn't be happier with the artwork! Thanks, Peter! And thanks to designer Marissa Raybuck for the super fun look of this book.

The long road from idea to publication wouldn't have happened without the advice and encouragement from my Middle Grade Mojo critique partners: Lisa Lewis Tyre, Debbie D'Aurelio, Lela Bridgers, Kevin Springer, Alison Hertz, Sherry Ellis, Kristine Anderson, and Danny Schnitzlein. I also learned so much from conferences and workshops hosted by Southern Breeze, our regional chapter of SCBWI. So, I'd like to thank all the dedicated people who volunteer their time to make those events happen.

A special thanks to Nora McFarland, who has been with me every step of my writing journey, and for telling me years ago, "Quit talking about it and do it!"

Thanks to my mom, Rita Hackler, who always believed I could do it . . . no matter what "it" was.

Even though he's not with us anymore, I'd like to thank my dad, Dean Hackler, for patiently answering my incessant questions when I was little. He would've enjoyed this book. I got my taste for trivia from him.

Thanks to Abby and Josie, for listening to me jabber on and on about fascinating food facts that probably weren't that fascinating to them. If I was boring them, they didn't let it show.

Most important, thanks to my husband, Dan, who has supported my writing career in countless ways. He happens to be an excellent copy editor as well.

Index

A

Africa, peanuts and, 78
Alexander the Great, 41
American foods. *See also
        individual foods*
        influences on, 1, 6
American Girl, The (magazine),
        97. *See also* Girl Scouts
American Heart Association
        (AHA), 12, 72
Anderson, Alexander Pierce,
        118–119
Ann Arbor Cookbook, The
        (Ladies' Aid Society), 26
Arend, Rene, 73
Asia, 31
        peanuts and, 78
Atlantic Peanut Refinery, 81
automobiles. *See also*
        Ford, Henry
        hamburgers and, 9–11, 12
Avayou, David, 46
Aztecs
        chocolate and the, 101–104,
        112
        Spanish explorers and the,
        15, 103–104

B

Baby Ruth bar (chocolate),
        110, 111
bacteria, 5, 52, 61. *See also
        E. coli*
Baker, James, 105
Baker, Robert, 71–72, 73

Baker's Company, 105
Barnum, P. T., 78
Barnum's Animal Cookies,
        95, 99
baseball
        hot dogs and, 52, 55–56
        peanuts and, 79
Bayle, George A., 80–81
Belgium, 18, 19
Birdseye, Clarence, 34
*Boston Cooking School
        Magazine of Culinary
        Science and Domestic
        Economics*, 85
*Brave Tart: Iconic American
        Desserts* (Parks), 96
bread. *See* sliced bread
Burger King (hamburgers), 11

C

Carlucci, Joe, 36
Carter, Jimmy, 87
Carver, George Washington, 81
cereals, 113–124. *See also
        individuals; individual
        brands*
        advertisements and, 120–121,
        122, 123
        children and, 121, 122
        China and, 114
        Europe and, 114
        experiment with, 115–116,
        118–119
        history of, 113–116
        milk and, 121
        nutrition and, 123
        sanitariums and, 113–115,
        118
        St. Louis World's Fair and,
        119

        sugar and, 116, 122, 123
        vitamins and, 121, 123, 124
Cheerios (cereal), 120, 123, 124
cheeses, 31, 36. *See also* pizzas
chickens, 62–76. *See also* eggs;
        individuals; Kentucky
        Fried Chicken (KFC);
        McDonald's
        American consumption of,
        62, 68, 75
        broilers and, 69–70
        Chicken Crispies, 71–72
        chicken fingers and nuggets,
        71–72, 73–74, 75, 76
        Chicken McNuggets, 73–74,
        75
        chicken soup, 66
        China and, 75
        fried chicken, 66–67, 70
        gluten-free recipe and, 76
        heart disease and, 72
        jungle fowl, 63–64
        nutrition and, 75
        royalty and, 75
        slaves and, 66–67
        vitamins and, 68–69, 75
children
        cereals and, 121, 122
        vitamins and, 121
Chillicothe Baking Company, 84
China
        cereals and, 114
        chickens and, 75
        cookies and, 99
chocolate, 101–112. *See also
        individuals; individual
        brands*
        American consumption of,
        107–110, 111
        Aztecs and, 101–104, 112

cacao and, 101–103, 104, 105, 111

Central America and, 101, 103–104

Columbian Exposition (1893) and, 107

early companies and, 105

Europe and, 104–105

J. S. Fry & Sons and, 105

milk chocolate, 90, 105–106, 108, 111

name origins and, 104

nutrition and, 111

oil and water and, 106

recipes for, 112

Spanish explorers and, 78, 103–104

the Swiss and, 111

when bars debuted, 105

World Wars and, 109

chocolate chip cookies

brands of, 91

Massachusetts and, 89, 92

National Chocolate Chip Cookie Day, 99

Nestlé (company) and, 91

Wakefield, Ruth and, 89–90

World War II and, 91

coconut. *See* macaroons

Columbian Exchange

definition of, 15

Spanish explorers and, 14–15

Columbian Exposition (1893)

chocolate and the, 107

hot dogs and the, 53

Columbus, Christopher, 14

condiments. *See also* ketchup; mustard

French fries and, 20

hamburgers and, 12

St. Louis World's Fair and, 46, 53

cookies, 89–100. *See also individual names of cookies*

China and, 99

colonists and, 92–93

Dutch immigrants and, 92–93

Egypt and, 92

Girl Scouts and, 97–98

Loose-Wiles Biscuit Company/Sunshine Biscuits and, 96

National Biscuit Company (Nabisco) and, 95, 96, 98

nutrition and, 99

origins of, 92

peanut butter and, 88

Persia (Iran) and, 92

sugar and, 94–95

world records and, 99

World War II and, 91, 98

Corn Flakes (cereal), 117, 118, 120, 123

Corn Pops (cereal), 120

Cortés, Hernán, 103–104. *See also* Spanish explorers

cotton candy, 46

Crosby, Alfred W., 15

Crum, George, 20–22

D

dachshunds (dogs), 55, 56

Davis, Fletcher (Old Dave), 9

Dietary Guidelines for Americans, sugar and, 99

Dorgan, Thomas A., 56

Do-si-dos (cookies), 98

doughnuts, 94

Doumar, Abe, 46

Dr Pepper (soda), 46

Dutch immigrants, 92–94

cookies and, 92–93

Native Americans and, 93

E

E. coli (*Escherichia coli*), 5

eggs, 63–65, 75

allergies to, 86

Egypt and, 64–65

English colonists and, 65

winter and, 68, 69

Egypt, ancient

cookies and, 92

eggs and, 64–65

Elizabeth, Queen, 58–59

Escherich, Theodor, 5

Europe. *See also individual countries*

cereals and, 114

chocolate and, 104–105

F

Ferry chip cookers, 22–23

Feuchtwanger, Anton, 53

Fig Newtons (cookies), 92, 99

Food and Drug Administration (FDA)

meat and the, 5

vitamins and the, 121

Ford, Henry, 10

France

ice cream and, 41–42

potatoes and, 16, 18, 19, 20

French fries, 18–20. *See also individuals*; potatoes
    annual American consumption and, 25
    condiments and, 20
    as most suitable to fry, 19
    nutrition and, 25
    restaurants, drive-ins and, 10, 19
    World War II and, 19
Frischman, Ignatz, 53
Fritos, 24
Frosted Flakes (cereal), 120, 121
frozen foods, 33–34. *See also* Birdseye, Clarence
Funk, Casmir, 68

G

Gallus gallus. *See* jungle fowl
General Mills (company), 120, 123
Genghis Khan, 2–3, 4
George VI, King, 58–59
Germany
    chocolate and, 111
    hamburgers and, 4–6, 12
    hot dogs and, 6, 50, 52, 55
    immigration to America from, 6, 17, 52, 55
    potatoes and, 6, 16, 17, 20
gingersnaps (cookies), 94
Girl Scouts, 97–98. *See also individual Girl Scout cookies*
Gluten-free recipes
    chicken nuggets, 76
    peanut butter cookies, 88
    potato chips, 26
Granola (cereal), 115, 118

Granula (cereal), 115
Grape-Nuts (cereal), 118, 120
Guthrie's restaurants, 74

H

Hallauer, George, 45
Hamburg (Germany), 6. *See also* Germany
Hamburg as city name, 8
Hamburger Charlie. *See* Nagreen, Charlie (Hamburger Charlie)
hamburgers, 2–13. *See also individuals*; *individual brands*
    annual festivals and, 7
    automobiles and, 9–11
    condiments for, 12
    Germany and, 4–6, 12
    history of, 2–6
    nutrition and, 12
    patties on buns and, 7–11
    recipe for, 13
    restaurants, drive-ins and, 9–11
    Russia and, 4
    St. Louis World's Fair, 9, 46
    Wisconsin and, 7
    world records and, 12
Hamwi, Ernest, 46
Handwerker, Nathan, 60
Hanon, John, 105
heart disease, 12, 25, 72, 87, 111
Heinz company, 20
Hershey, Milton, 107–108
Hershey bars (chocolate), 108, 110, 111
Honey Smacks (cereal), 120
hot dogs, 50–61. *See also individuals*

annual American consumption and, 60
baseball and, 55–56
buns and, 53
Columbian Exposition (1893) and, 53
dachshunds (dogs) and, 55, 56
Germany and, 6, 50, 52, 55
how they are made, 56–58, 59
immigration to America and, 6, 52
meat preservation and, 52
mustard and, 53–54
name origins and, 54–55
Nathan's Famous hot dogs, 60
nutrition and, 59, 60
Roman Empire and, 50, 51
royalty and, 58–59
St. Louis World's Fair and, 46, 53
Howard Johnson's (Hojo's), 40
hydrogenation, peanut butter and, 82–83, 87
Hydrox (cookies), 96

I

ice boxes, 44
ice cream, 39–49. *See also individuals*
    American history and, 42–46
    bars and, 47
    flavors and, 47
    France and, 41–42
    Italy and, 41
    nutrition and, 48
    Persia (Iran) and, 40–41
    recipe for, 43, 49
    restaurant chains and, 47
    salt and, 42
    songs and, 40

St. Louis World's Fair and,
    45–46
toppings and, 45
world history and, 40–42
world records and, 48
ice cream cones. *See also*
    individuals
    multiple independent
        discovery and, 45–46
immigration to America
    Germany and, 6, 17, 52, 55
    hot dogs and, 6, 52
    Ireland and, 17
    pizzas and, 31
    potatoes and, 17, 18
    town names and, 8
In-N-Out (restaurant), 10
inventions and discoveries.
    See also individual foods
    multiple independent
        discovery, 1, 45–46
Iran. *See* Persia (Iran)
Ireland
    chocolate and, 111
    immigration to America and,
        17
    potatoes and, 16–17
iron, 121, 124
Italy. *See also individuals*;
    Naples (Italy); Roman
    Empire
    ice cream and, 41
    pizzas and, 27–31

J

Jackson, James Caleb, 114, 115.
    See also Seventh-day
    Adventists
Jackson, Reuben W., 10

jams and jellies, 85–86, 87.
    See also PB&J
    science of, 86
    Welch family and, 85
Jefferson, Thomas
    French fries and, 18
    ice cream and, 43
    peanuts and, 87
Johnson, Howard, 40
Johnson, Nancy B., 43
J. S. Fry & Sons, chocolate and,
    105
jungle fowl (*Gallus gallus*),
    63–64

K

Kabbaz, Nick, 46
Kellogg, John Harvey, 80, 87,
    113–118
Kellogg, Will Keith, 113–118
    as businessman, 116–118
    as marketer, 120–121
Kellogg brothers
    conflict between the, 113,
        116–117
    flakes and the, 115–116
    peanut butter and the, 80
    sanitariums and the, 80,
        114–115, 116, 118
    as Seventh-day Adventists,
        114
    sugar and the, 114, 116
Kellogg's Company, 117–118,
    120–121, 123
Kentucky Fried Chicken (KFC),
    70, 73, 74
ketchup, 12. *See also* condiments
    origins of, 20
Kirby, J. G., 10

Kix (cereal), 120
Kroc, Ray, 73. *See also*
    McDonald's
Kublai Khan, 4

L

Lassen, Louis, 8–9
Lay, Herman, 24
Lay's Potato Chips, 24
Linnaeus, Carl von, 111
Lombardi, Gennaro, 31
Loose, Jacob, 96
Loose-Wiles Biscuit Company,
    96
Louis' Lunch, 8–9. *See also*
    Lassen, Louis

M

M&M's (chocolate), 109
macaroons (cookies), 94
    recipes for, 100
Madison, James and Dolley, 43
Margherita, Queen (Italy),
    30–31. *See also* Umberto,
    King (Italy)
Mars, Frank and Forrest, 109
Massachusetts, chocolate chip
    cookies and, 89, 92
McDonald's, 11, 12, 70
    chickens and, 73–74
Meat Inspection Act (1906), 5
meat preservation, 50, 52, 60
Menches, Charles and Frank
    hamburgers and the, 7–8
    ice cream and the, 46
Mexico
    Cortés, Hernán and, 103–104
    potatoes and, 20

Mayer, Oscar, 57
milk, 48, 86, 89, 111
 cereals and, 121, 123
milk chocolate, 90, 105–106,
  108, 111. *See also* chocolate
Milky Way (chocolate), 109, 111
molasses, 94
Morse, Samuel, 29
Mr. Potato Head, 25
Mrs. Rorer's New Cook Book: A
  Manual of Housekeeping
  (Rorer)
 hamburgers and, 13
 macaroons and, 100
multiple independent discovery
 definition of, 1
 ice cream cones and, 45–46
Murrie, Bruce, 109
mustard
 as condiment, 54, 60
 hamburgers and, 12
 hot dogs and, 53–54, 56
 recipe for, 61
 St. Louis World's Fair and,
  46, 53

N

Nagreen, Charlie (Hamburger
  Charlie), 7
Naples (Italy), 28–31. *See also*
  Italy
 Pizzeria Brandi and, 30–31
 True Neapolitan Pizza
  Association and, 36
Nathan's Famous hot dogs, 60
National Biscuit Company
  (Nabisco), 95, 96, 99
Native Americans
 Dutch immigrants and, 93
 Spanish explorers and, 15

Nero, Emperor of Rome, 41
Nestlé (company), 91
Nestlé, Henri, 106
New-York Tribune, 9
Noss, Harvey, 24
nutrition. *See Dietary*
  Guidelines for Americans;
  vitamins; *individual foods*

O

Old Dave. *See* Davis, Fletcher
  (Old Dave)
Oreo cookies, 96, 99

P

Panapoulos, Sam, 35
Parks, Stella, 96
PB&J, 83–86, 87
 annual American
  consumption and, 86, 87
 jams and jellies and, 85–86
 nutrition and, 86, 87
 World Wars and, 85–86
peanut butter, 77–88. *See also*
  individuals; individual
  brands
 annual American
  consumption and, 86, 87
 Atlantic Peanut Refinery, 81
 brands of, 82
 cookies and, 88
 gluten-free cookie recipe
  and, 88
 hydrogenation and, 82–83, 87
 Kellogg brothers and, 80
 as legume, 77
 nutrition and, 80, 86, 87
 origins of, 80–81
 PB&J and, 83–86

peanut plant, 77–78, 81
 sliced bread and, 83
 Spanish explorers and, 78
 St. Louis World's Fair and,
  46, 81–82
Peanut Promoter, The (trade
  journal), 80
peanuts, 77–79, 80, 86, 87.
  See also individuals
 Africa and, 78
 allergies to, 86
 alternative names for, 87
 Asia and, 78
 baseball and, 79
 circuses and, 78
 slaves and, 78
 South America and, 78
Penn, William, 6
Pennsylvania. *See* Hershey,
  Milton
pepperoni, 32, 36
Persia (Iran)
 cookies and, 92
 ice cream and, 40–41
Peru, potatoes and, 14
Peter, Daniel, 106
Peter Pan (peanut butter), 82, 87
Pizzaro, Francisco, 14
pizzas, 27–38. *See also*
  individuals
 annual American
  consumption and, 27
 cheeses and, 31
 as frozen food, 33–34
 immigration to America and,
  31
 Italy and, 27–31
 nutrition and, 36
 pepperoni and, 32
 recipe for, 37–38

regional styles of, 35
restaurant chains and, 33
royalty and, 30–31
tomatoes and, 28–29, 36
True Neapolitan Pizza
Association and, 36
world records and, 36
World War II and, 33
Pizzeria Brandi, 30–31
Poland. *See* Prussia (Poland)
Post, C. W., 118
as marketer, 120
Post Toasties (cereal), 118
potato chips. *See also*
individuals; individual
brands
invention of, 20–22
mass production of, 22–23
nutrition and, 25
recipe for, 26
Saratoga chips, 22
why they go stale, 23
world records and, 25
World War II and, 24
potatoes, 14–26. *See also*
French fries; potato chips
annual American
consumption and, 19, 25
famines and, 17
France and, 16, 18, 19, 20
Germany and, 6, 16, 17, 20
Great Britain and, 20
immigration to America and,
17, 18
Ireland and, 16–17
Mexico and, 20
nutrition and, 25
Peru and, 14
potato blight and, 17
Prussia (Poland) and, 16

Russia and, 16
Spanish explorers and, 14–15
world records and, 25
Prussia (Poland), 16
puffed cereals, 46, 119, 120
Puffed Rice cereal, 119

Q

Quaker Oats Company (Quaker
Foods), 119, 123

R

Randolph, Mary, 67
Riccardo, Ric, 35
Rice Krispies (cereal), 120, 121
Rohwedder, Otto Frederick,
sliced bread and, 83–84
Roman Empire, 28, 41, 50, 51, 66.
See also Nero, Emperor
of Rome
hot dogs and the, 50, 51
Roosevelt, Franklin D. and
Eleanor, 58–59
Rorer, Sarah Tyson, 13, 100
Rosefield, Joseph, 82
Russia
hamburgers and, 4
potatoes and, 16

S

Samoas (cookies), 98
Sanders, Harland, 70. *See also*
Kentucky Fried Chicken
(KFC)
sanitariums, 80, 114–115,
116, 118
Saratoga chips, 22. *See also*
potato chips

Bayle, George A. and, 81
recipes for, 26
Schnering, Otto, 110
Scudder, Laura, 23
Seventh-day Adventists.
See also Jackson, James
Caleb
beliefs of, 114, 115, 116
Kellogg brothers as, 114, 116
sugar and, 114, 116
Sewell, Ike, 35
shortbread (cookie), 94, 98
Skippy (peanut butter), 82
slaves
chickens and, 66–67
peanuts and, 78
sliced bread
Chillicothe Baking Company
and, 84
peanut butter and, 83, 85
Rohwedder, Otto Frederick
and, 83–84
Snickers bar (chocolate), 109,
111
Snyder, Harry and Esther, 10
South America, peanuts and, 78
Spanish explorers. *See also*
Cortés, Hernán
Aztecs and, 15, 103–104
chocolate and, 78, 103–104
Columbian Exchange and,
14–15
food introductions and,
14–15, 29, 78, 103–104
native populations and, 15
peanut butter and, 78
potatoes and, 14–15
tomatoes and, 15, 29, 78
vanilla and, 78
Stevens, Harry, 56

St. Louis World's Fair
  cereals and the, 119
  condiments and the, 46, 53
  hamburgers and the, 9, 46
  hot dogs and the, 46, 53
  ice cream and the, 45–46
  peanut butter and the, 46, 81–82
Stockton, Frank, 82
sugar
  cereals and, 116, 122, 123
  cookies and, 94–95
  Dietary Guidelines for Americans and, 99
  Kellogg brothers and, 114
  nutrition and, 99, 123
  Seventh-day Adventists and, 114, 116
Sumner, C. H., 81
Swiss, the, chocolate and, 106, 111

T
Tagalongs (cookies), 98
Texas Pig Stand, 10
Thin Mints (cookies), 98
tomatoes
  pizzas and, 28–29, 36
  Spanish explorers and, 15, 29, 78
Tried and True Cookbook (Wakefield), 90
True Neapolitan Pizza Association, 36
Turner, Fred, 73

U
Umberto, King (Italy), 30. *See also* Margherita, Queen (Italy)
United Kingdom, 20, 25, 58–59, 93
  chocolate and the, 111

V
Van Houten, Coenraad, 105
vanilla, 47
  Spanish explorers and, 15, 78
Varsity, The, 12
vegetarian diets, 80, 114, 115
Virginia Housewife, The (Randolph), 67
vitamins
  cereals and, 121, 123, 124
  chickens and, 68–69, 75
  children and, 121
  Food and Drug Administration (FDA) and, 121

W
Wakefield, Ruth, 89–91
Welch family, 85. *See also* jams and jellies
Wendy's (hamburgers), 11
Wheaties (cereal), 123
White Castle (hamburgers), 9
Wicks, Katie, 20, 22
Wiles, John, 96
Williams, Ansley, 74

Wisconsin, hamburgers and, 7
world records. *See individual foods*
World War I
  chocolate and, 109
  PB&J and, 85
World War II
  chocolate and, 109
  cookies and, 91, 98
  French fries and, 19
  PB&J and, 86
  pizzas and, 33
  potato chips and, 24

Y
Yarbrough, Alben and Dusty, 74